FROM THE BACK OF THE HOUSE

Memories of a Steak House Clan

Gary L. Rockey

HERITAGE BOOKS
2009

HERITAGE BOOKS
AN IMPRINT OF HERITAGE BOOKS, INC.

Books, CDs, and more—Worldwide

For our listing of thousands of titles see our website at
www.HeritageBooks.com

Published 2009 by
HERITAGE BOOKS, INC.
Publishing Division
100 Railroad Ave. #104
Westminster, Maryland 21157

Copyright © 2009 Gary L. Rockey

All rights reserved. No part of this book may be reproduced or transmitted in any form or by any means, electronic or mechanical, including photocopying, recording or by any information storage and retrieval system without written permission from the author, except for the inclusion of brief quotations in a review.

International Standard Book Numbers
Paperbound: 978-0-7884-4916-1
Clothbound: 978-0-7884-8165-9

FROM THE BACK OF THE HOUSE

Special thanks to Evelyn Rose*, Les Roberts, Cheri Rourke, Mary Vins Roll, Tom Stickney, Bill Barrow, and most of all, Concetta.

---

* Evelyn Rose (1922-2009) after a long struggle with breathing problems (she was on oxygen, probably related to years of smoking and breathing beauty salon fumes) passed away January 27, 2009. She would have been eighty-seven on February 6 and looked forward to reading this book. She did get to see some of it before it went to the publisher and, of course, for the most part lived it.

FROM THE BACK OF THE HOUSE - permissions

© 1959, 1960,1966, 1967, 1969, 1974, 1975, 1984, 1987, 1995, 1997 The Plain Dealer. All rights reserved. Used with permission of The Plain Dealer.

Cleveland Press Collection, used with permission of the Cleveland State University Library

" . . . arriving at a larger truth about families . . . there is no self-pity, no whining, no hunger for revenge . . . we are not victims . . . we come from a tribe of fallible people . . .and we have endured to tell the story without judgement and to get on with our lives."
Inventing the Truth . . . William Zinsser

INTRODUCTION

by

Les Roberts*

When I was down on Collision Bend, on the industrial west bank of the Flats in Cleveland, doing research for my forthcoming book of the same title, I dropped into Jim's Steak House for a quick beer one raw spring afternoon. I had no idea I was opening a brand-new box of memories. I'd had dinner at Jim's a few times before, and from the dining room I always enjoyed watching the 600-foot ore boats glide past on Cuyahoga River, seemingly so close I could reach out and touch them.

But the small, intimate bar at the back of the house was a different world. I began a relationship with one of my best friends, public relations maven Ron Watt, and for the next several years we whiled away many afternoons at that bar that sometimes stretched into the evening, beginning with lunch of a steak sandwich and home fries that tasted better than I'd eaten anywhere else. Sure, it was a heart attack on a plate, but the enjoyment of it, along with excellent drinks poured by one of the greatest bartenders I've ever known, the late Ray Macaskee.

I met the most interesting people who hung out in that little bar more often than I did. Some were industrialists and corporate CEOs, some were reporters, and cops, laborers, a few dedicated imbibers, and a regular group of men who always lunched there with attractive women who weren't their wives. There was always someone fun to talk with. The small TV that always played quietly at the end of the bar was generally ignored by everyone except when something fascinating happened news-wise and we all pounced on it for a spirited conversation.

It took me such a short time to become so enamored of Jim's Steak House and the atmosphere it provided that was so . . . Cleveland . . . that I moved the office of my series protagonist, Cleveland private eye Milan Jacovich, from the front room of his apartment to a nonexistent building right next to Jim's, so he could drop in there and have fictional lunches as often as I had real ones. The real building right next door is a warehouse, hardly a fit place for anyone to have an office, but it doesn't fit the fictional description I bestowed on it in the books, because JIM'S Steak House deserved a classy and atmospheric neighbor, even if it was only on paper.

I came along too late in my newborn Cleveland life to ever visit the elegant apartment upstairs, the one boasting the most sweeping view of downtown, but hardly a week went past that I didn't fantasize about it and yearn to one day live there. How amazing it must be to wake up every morning and look out the window at the close-by Cuyahoga River, the swooping gulls, the rush hour traffic patterns swirling around Jacobs Field, and the colorful Cleveland bridges.

Sadly for my novels, and for a whole trainload of its former habitués, Jim's Steak House closed a few years later. Now Milan Jacovich has to find somewhere else to eat, even as he pines for what used to be. So do I. While I've found other places to enjoy a midday meal, like Johnny's Bar on Fulton and its younger bother downtown, Swingos on the Lake, and my new particular favorite, the venerable Ferris Steak House on Detroit Road, the ambiance is never quite the same. There is a wry hole in my sentimental heart where Jim's Steak House used to be.

---

*Les Roberts is the author of numerous novels including, set in Cleveland, his Milan Jacovich mystery series. In his recent memoir from Gray Publishing, "We'll Always Have Cleveland," he recounts his Jim's Steak House experience.

PREFACE

Pittsburgh Pennsylvania native, Hilda Theresa Hoffman (alias Aunt Hilda, Mrs. Jim's, The Queen of the Flats, Tootsie), before it was popular for women to more than cook, hand-wash clothes and hang the wet laundry on an outside line, built Cleveland's Jim's Steak House into a landmark restaurant.

Mrs JIM'S

The soothsayers didn't know it then, but in Hilda breathed the precursor of the women's movement. Aunt Hilda, in spirit and size, a formidable woman (bare feet around 5' 11', weighing in at 200 give or take pounds), was somebody you'd like to have at your side at night in a dark alley.

A make-things-happen gal when go-to gals were rare as oyster short hairs, Hilda let you know where you stood, could go, or end up. She was known to throw things at people who displeased her.

Witness my sixteenth birthday. I was going out of town to visit relatives in Pennsylvania. Minutes before departing,

Aunt Hilda came looming through the doorway, threw a wrapped gift at me, said, "Here's your goddamn birthday present, you have to spoil everything." Tearing up, she turned and left.

The let-you-know prowess sometimes bled over to JIM'S dinner guests. One episode had Hilda hosting dinner when in walked a famous Hollywood lady movie star of the fifties. The lady, in addition to being a silver screen star, had won a gold medal in Olympic swimming. The movie star and a friend told Hilda they wished to be seated in an intimate dinning nook off the main dining room called the PD (Private Dining). Hilda informed the couple, "The PD is closed." The famous star insisted, wanted to be seated in that "lovely quiet little room." Hilda said again, "It's closed." The star's friend said, "But perhaps you don't know who this is." Hilda declared, "I don't give a damn who she is, that room is closed." Star and friend left.

Maybe that's why some called Hilda a "diamond in the rough." Whatever and for sure, beneath the slurry and expletives deleted, glittered what the Jim's Steak House menu proclaimed for decades about the Cuyahoga "... down where her heart beats, she's pure and unsullied ..."

In short, the venerable Mrs. JIM, for some sixty years, fed, hosted, coddled, and dusted off sailors, scallywags and statesmen from far and wide. And after the dust settled, she began a novena.

Orphaned at four when his mother died, Aunt Hilda's nephew (she called him "my boy" he called her Tootsie) was none other than Raymond Charles Rockey. To JIM'S patrons, employees, and pals, bells may be going off. To others, Ray began working at *the* Steak House from the time his voice started changing at around eight. He remained there until his final voice change (as in stopped) a few weeks prior to his seventy-second birthday. Ray stood in at about 5' 7", weighed around 160 pounds, parted his slicked black hair high on the left. Bob Seltzer of *The Cleveland Press* * saw him this way: " . . . a slender, businesslike man of equanimity and penetrating insight into the multiple facets of a [restaurant]." (*Cleveland Press*, November 19, 1968)

Jim's Steak House Manager, Ray (circa 1955) having a JIM'S lunch

Ray's pet line when talking about JIM'S, the words flowing off his lips like honeyed tea, "It's a baby that never grows up," were chiseled in his psyche. And he (never sick, never, hung over maybe) nursed Jim's Steak House 24/7.

Hosting JIM'S dinner hour (his favorite job), he was always manicured to a T in tailored suit, white shirt, and Windsor Knot just so. Greeting customers with a toothy gap-between-incisors' smile, seating them, he presented menus to each with, "The special of the night is (fill in the blank)," capping it off with "And the steaks better be good."

Laughing in little "ha ha's," his panache brought them back to dine and drink again and again. He favored the direct approach in matters' amour, seldom used the F word, sprinkled a *Jesus Christ* and *God Damn* around, with a heady *son of a bitch* thrown in for good measure. His favorite movie *Casablanca* (Bogart as Rick, running Rick's Café, his idol) might explain some things. Which ones, aside from smoking, drinking, and paramours, there are too many to count.

In Shakespear's, "As You Like It," Jacques laments that all the world's a stage with players passing through various ages from infancy to sans teeth, sans eyes, sans taste, sans everything. Ray's baby analogy in mind, JIM'S went through a few of these ages but for the most part (I have a suspicion all restaurants are), it was stuck in that first stage, the "baby" stage Ray Rockey mouthed.

Baby or not, Jim's Steak House the setting where Ray performed center stage for some fifty years, the stage analogy fits.

Like the star in a hit show, Ray found it heady being the lead on a popular restaurant's stage–whiffs of attention from perfumed dolls (some guys too), faux fame, recognition, the groupies coming out of the French dressing to dance on some forgotten bliss.

JIM'S was much more to others–that thing that hangs

bought. If you have to name it, it means nothing.

Stage, "baby," or no, one thing's for sure–to be successful in the restaurant business you have to (some would say absolutely must) do one thing–like people. The short, the fat, the tall and the in-between, Ray Rockey liked them all–tops, sides, and bottoms. When you entered JIM'S, Ray hosting, that what-ever-it-is that can't be faked, oozed from him like sap from some just tapped Douglas fir. One in ten thousand is cut out for the restaurant racket. Next time you go out to dine, look for it, you'll get the gist.

---

* See *The Cleveland Press* end note #1

PART I

MYTHS AND BEGINNINGS

Jim's STEAK HOUSE

1

LINGO & FIRST IMPRESSIONS

Restaurant people (managers, employees, owners, refer to the dinning, drinking, cocktail lounging areas of a restaurant as "the front of the house." They call the kitchen (where cooks' cook, dishwashers wash, servers place orders, the restaurant staff, including the manager let it all hang out) "the back of the house."

JIM'S circa 1948

This is a "back of the house" stroll down a memory lane of the family who owned, operated, and lived (through a half century and a dozen remodeling jobs) above Cleveland's famous landmark restaurant, Jim'S Steak House.

Strolls and such down memory lanes often equated with

FROM THE BACK OF THE HOUSE

bovine watch-your-step stuff, some might see JIM'S differently. Many walked in the front door. I walked through the back door.

It was 1950, nine years old (I would be adopted four years later by Ray Rockey) when that back door led me into JIM'S cavernous kitchen where, like into a brewing vat of forever, first impressions stuck:

Tooth and toothless male faces (black and white), some smiling, others with a "who are you" look, studied me. Some of them dressed in checkered breeches and short sleeve shirts, I later learned these people were "scullers." A.k.a. dishwashers, general kitchen help. One sculler mopped the cream-colored floor-tile with a grease cutting witch's brew that iced my nose membrane. Another brushed by and opened a metal-hinged thick wooden door which led to a walk-in cooler where mountains of boiled potatoes, sliced onions, and gallons of bottled salad dressing sat on metal racks. I later learned there was another walk-in cooler where racks of raw meat was stored.

Moving further into the kitchen environs, were two dinosaur looking black stoves (broilers and ovens) behind which, moving like lion tamers, were two cooks wearing spattered aprons and white paper hats.

Weaving and winding in and about it all were women (the waitresses, at JIM'S called "girls") in white uniforms and white shoes. They beaming down at me like a good size tuna

FROM THE BACK OF THE HOUSE

that had just been hauled onboard a fishing boat.

Binding the impressions were the sharp and flats of dishes being stacked, a meat saw whanging its way through prime beef, and a cacophony of chatter, chit chat, and yelps.

And in it all, there breathed close by, an aura, another presence, like a smell you're not quite sure of.

I didn't know it then (no one knows it then), but I was entering one of those unknown zones that changes who you are, where black and white are in betweens and nothing is forever. In short, an interesting ride had begun, some ups, some downs, always the thrill of what they call living. But like all living, the longer you get into it the more you wonder.

Anyway, memories like the hole in a glazed donut, I was there–back, front, upstairs, in the basement–for a good part of the Jim's Steak House run, sometimes from a distance, more than not up close. The early years were good, sweet actually, maybe too good. The end . . . eh.

2
MIFFS, MYTHS, AND DIALOGUE

In 1995, after Ray Rockey went on to the big restaurant in the sky, the family took over and I got to be manager. More on that later but for now, one of my manager perks was answering the JIM'S phone. Five out of ten calls involved giving driving direction to people who weren't sure how to get to the restaurant. It went something like:

ME: Hello, Jim's Steak House
CALLER: Where you located?
ME: 1800 Scranton Road, at Collision Bend, Cuyahoga River, the Flats.
CALLER: How do I get there?
ME: Where are you coming from?
CALLER: East, coming down Carnegie.
ME: Turn off Carnegie onto Huron, going west, turn onto Eagle Ramp, bottom of the ramp, just over the draw bridge, right side, next to the fire station, corner of Carter street and Scranton Road, big red JIM'S neon sign on top, can't miss it.
CALLER: Eagle Ramp is open now?
ME: Yes. (The Eagle Bridge and Ramp are now closed "permanently" [2008] but that's for later.)
CALLER: That bridge is broke.
ME: No, the bridge is fixed now . . . Eagle Ramp is open.
CALLER: You can't take a right off of Carnegie.
ME: Yes you can, just turn right off Carnegie . . .

FROM THE BACK OF THE HOUSE

CALLER: You can't.

ME: Take a right at the light and come down Eagle Ramp over the Eagle bridge.

CALLER: That bridge is closed.

ME: No, it's not.

CALLER: It was.

ME: Not now.

CALLER: What's that other bridge?

ME: What other bridge.

CALLER: The one that goes up and down.

ME: I thought you ask how to get here.

Many times listening to Ray Rockey give similar directions to would-be customers (Ray knew every street, alley, building, bridge, and bump in all the Flat's roads and byways) I imagined ancient Chippewa telling visiting debutantes which dirt paths to take through the Flats. And in Ray's case, the debutantes better be home before dark.

Closed Sundays, Christmas and Thanksgiving, JIM'S otherwise opened its door, 11:00 a.m., Monday through Saturday, fifty two weeks a year since forever or at least since 1940. In another sense open all the time, the topic–if not on the top, sniffing around just below the surface of every family gathering–was JIM'S.

In conversations around the breakfast, lunch, dinner table, watching TV, at family reunions, birthday parties,

FROM THE BACK OF THE HOUSE

riding in a car, on the telephone, in bed, whatever, it was always first things first as in, "How'd we do last night," (translation what was the take in dollars and cents). Alter than, top of the list talk centered on the employees, otherwise known as the "help"–sick, healthy, getting good ones and keeping them, the bartender's stealing, a cook's cut thumb, a waitresses' son graduating.

Following that, talk could go anywhere–who was doing what to whom in the restaurant/bar business around town, a newspaper food critic's review, a new joint opening, the cost of beef, or a drunk customer falling asleep at the bar.

Occasionally the talk turned to mundane things–cleaning grease traps, repairing coolers, paying vendors, mopping the floor, steaming kettles of potatoes (boiled with jackets on) to be chopped for hash browns, beef fat rendering, batter for onion rings, thousand island dressing, shining of flatware, men's and ladies' room towels, sewer backed up, roof leaking, basement flooded again, grass needing cut.

Sometime the talk got specific, "Bookkeeper is sick, won't be in."

"Caught Pete going out the back door with three New York strips under his coat, fired him."

"Somebody, at lunch yesterday, said the flower beds (In the spring, at flower planting parties, Ray drank Amstel light and watched the "girls" plant flowers on, around, and at the

FROM THE BACK OF THE HOUSE

sides of JIM'S lawn) aren't what they used to be."

"Man complained last night that we didn't have butter patties like we used to."

"Woman called, said she sat by the door to the kitchen, heard swearing and yelling, just awful."

"That dentist, what's his name, was in last night, said the hash browns aren't nice and golden brown like they used to be."

"City health inspector was in, have to do something with the knife drawer."

"Gas meter man couldn't get in to read the meter (The meter was in the basement, if he came when the door was locked he guessed), he estimated!"

"Man said his T-bone was the best steak he ever had, loved the hash browns."

In and around all of the above talk, there most often came out of the blue: "I'm going to *the* Steak House." It was always THE steak house. Not JIM'S, the restaurant, home. Always, THE steak house. You knew it wasn't Broglios, or the Ground Round, or the Brown Derby, or whatever. It was THE steak house.

Regarding the "Man said his T-bone was the best he ever had . . . ," one compliment out of a hundred was savored, repeated, put in memory's notebook. On the other hand, gripes were remembered like an unwanted relative.

FROM THE BACK OF THE HOUSE

Speaking of compliments and gripes, it's funny, maybe not so funny, how some people are eager to complain while other are almost shy, reluctant to compliment. Maybe in today's world it's more macho to confront. Or maybe it's only which reality you choose to see, remember, look at.

Whatever and along the comment line, you often hear a couple, waiting for a table in a packed restaurant's lobby, whispering to one another. One of them, usually the male, says, "Honey, look at all these people, they must be making a fortune in this place. Let's open a restaurant. Your meat balls are divine, people would come from miles away, gobble them up. Sell 'em two bucks a piece!" Shaking his head, the male adds, "No wonder all these restaurant people have big cars, homes in Florida."

And so honey agrees, they do it, and the other shoe drops. Why do you think so many joints are like the lyrics in that song, "riding high in April, shot down in May?"

The proof in the shoe drop, seems every time I go to some exotic vacation spot, usually twice a year, a favorite restaurant is either closed or under new management with a new name, a new menu, and a new famous chef from New York.

Lists of varying sorts in vogue these days, following is a list of ten reasons not to go into the restaurant business, unless of course, you love the short the fat and the tall of

FROM THE BACK OF THE HOUSE

humanity. If you fall in the latter category, it's a list of reasons to take the plunge. But be careful. There are only a few unique-to-the-species, one in a million individuals (Ray Rockey was one) who actually thrive on this list's stuff. Ray basked in it, basted fat juices over himself in it, ate it. The more the better–short, fat, tall, rare, medium, well done, pink or just plain raw, he loved it.

The list:

NUMBER ONE–stomachs

When you deal with people's stomaches, you can understand why Darwin was right. People are animals. No doubt about it. When people are hungry, you could dangle kinky sex, a warm bed, gold bars under their nose and they would growl, look away. Mess with their spouse, their kids, anything, but mess with their stomachs, you're dead meat. Flip side, make stomachs feel good, you're God. Deny a stomach, you're evil, sinister, rude, up from the pit. It's kinda like a priest is to people's soul, in this case to their stomachs.

NUMBER TWO–recognition

Never own a restaurant unless you can be in Timbuktu when the joint is in your hometown. Even then you have to watch your step. Somebody asks you what you do and you say the name of your restaurant and nine out of ten, somebody has been in it and four to five this is the one out of ten that had a problem–food, service, drink, something got

FROM THE BACK OF THE HOUSE

screwed up. That reminds me of a joke I heard in a Las Vegas lounge. There's these three little old Italian ladies, they go to this fancy restaurant every week, same table, same seating arrangement, same everything. So this one night, served their main course, the owner goes up to the table and says, "Evening ladies, is *anything* okay."

There's another thing related to recognition. Sometimes when you own a restaurant you get confused because people come in and treat you like you're a celebrity. They call you by your first name, introduce you to friends, say things like: "I know the owner, Joe; Where's my buddy, Joe? ; Hey, is Joe in? ; Tell Joe I said hello; Have Joe come to our table."

Joe goes to their table and it's like the Pope has arrived, the Dalai Lama at least, like live TV, better yet taped. Everybody wants an autograph. And best of all, if it's an I-know-Joe guy on a first date, if Joe perchance goes to the table, the I-know-Joe guy gets (later on) lucky or better that night, hands down.

Bottom line, why do you think people are so proud they know Joe? It's not because they especially like Joe, it's because (Number One above) Joe can assuage their stomachs. Where do you think the saying, "never bite the hand that feeds you," came from? It goes way back before caves.

NUMBER THREE–rare

FROM THE BACK OF THE HOUSE

Take rare for instance. Rare has a thousand faces. People don't know rare from a red flag. Medium rare, medium well, a little on the rare side, medium, pink in the middle, cold in the middle. Pittsburgh rare (raw in the middle.):
"This isn't cooked."
" You said rare."
"I know, but I don't want to see any blood."
Well done is another thing. Well done, well done medium, no pink, no red, no blood:
"This is overcooked."
"You said well done."
" I didn't say burnt."
You could go on and on, press the fleshy part of your hand above your thumb, hold your nose, stick a fork in it . . . it's like "what is electricity" or "why is blue blue?"
NUMBER FOUR–booze

At the bar, a short fat bald guy with a tall shapely blond female (blond younger by at least 25 years) on his arm, the bald guy says: "Hey, wha-kin-a-gin you put in this martini?"
"Beefeaters."
"No iss not."
"Wanna bet."
"Lesss see the bottle."
"Ange, give me that bottle."
"I don care what it says, at's not Beefeaters in ere

FROM THE BACK OF THE HOUSE

martini."
 "Here's the bottle, what a ya want."
 "Probably put at cheap stuff in the Beefeater's bottle."
 He's wrong but wannayagonna do with a drunk, the only thing you can do: "Next one's on me."
 "Hiss is Tina."
 "Give her one too."
NUMBER FIVE–seating
 GUEST: Two, by the window.
 HOST: Be a half hour wait.
 GUEST: What about that table over there?
 HOST: Reserved.
 GUEST: What about that one?
 HOST: Reserved, I can give you that one, just a step form the window.
 GUEST: I don't see anybody waiting for the one by the window.
 HOST: They're on their way.
 GUEST: What about that one, over there.
 HOST: That's an eight top.
 GUEST: So?
 HOST: You're only two.
 GUEST: So? How about that one?
 HOST: Reserved.
 GUEST: That guy just left, I want his window table.

FROM THE BACK OF THE HOUSE

HOST: Reserved.
GUEST: For who?

NUMBER SIX–diners:
GUEST: Is this real butter?
HOST: Yep.
GUEST: No it's not.
HOST: Yes, it is, it's whipped.
GUEST: I liked it better when you had the real butter, not this whipped stuff. Doesn't even taste like butter.

GUEST: Sir, my son's salad has a fly in it.
HOST: That's extra.

GUEST: Say, why don't you put pasta on the menu.

GUEST: Hey, we've been waiting for an hour (two minutes) and haven't seen a waitress yet.

HOST: Smoking or non smoking?
GUEST: Smoking.
HOST: It's in the back.
GUEST: But we want to set by a window.
HOST: No can do.
GUEST: But I want to see the view.

FROM THE BACK OF THE HOUSE

HOST: Not if you want to smoke.
GUEST: How about cigars?

GUEST: You know, the salad was not real crispy tonight. And the hash browns used to be a golden brown, tell them not to burn them next time, and crisp up that lettuce.

GUEST: It's cold in here, can you turn the heat up.

GUEST: Hot in here, what's a matter, didn't you pay the electric bill?

GUEST: Say, we have the two for one Entertainment Coupon, could we just get the free one and split it?

GUEST: Say, I know how to make this a cash cow?
HOST: How?
GUEST: Topless.

GUEST: Could I get three pork chops, you serve only two, they're so little.

GUEST: Hey, how 'bout grind up some of your prize beef and make me a hamburger.

FROM THE BACK OF THE HOUSE

GUEST: What happened to the after dinner mints?

GUEST: (Burp)Got any toothpicks?

NUMBER SEVEN–telephone calls (in between the driving direction) throughout the day:
    ME: Hello Jim's Steak House.
    MALE: Hey, do you have pizza?

ME: Hello Jim's Steak House.
FEMALE: Say, I was in there last night for dinner and had diarrhea all night, I'm going to call an attorney.
ME: Did you have anything to drink with dinner?
FEMALE: Just a few glasses of red wine.
ME: That's what did it, red wine'll give you the green apple quick step every time.

ME: Hello Jim's Steak House.
MALE: Hey, this is Jack, I need a table for six, window, be in, half an hour.
ME: (Who the #"% is Jack!)

ME: Hello Jim's Steak House.
MALE: My wife is a vegetarian, do you serve vegetable plates?

FROM THE BACK OF THE HOUSE

ME: Hello Jim's Steak House.
MALE: Hey, this is Blue Ribbon Meats, you're over 90 days, when you gonna send a check?

ME: Hello, Jim's Steak House
MALE: This is the gas company, you're two months past due turn off time.

ME: Hello, Jim's Steak House
FEMALE: Hey, this is Betty, Wee Magazine, we have a special on advertising next week, full page for only a thousand bucks.

ME: Jim's Steak House
FISH MONGER: Hey Rock, I got fer you two cases Cod, seel em ya cheap.

ME: Jim's Steak House
BANK MANAGER: This is Provident bank, your overdrawn, five thousand.

NUMBER EIGHT–nitty gritty day to day stuff from staff:
"We need change, nickels and dimes. Need singles too. And don't forget, when you go to the bank, pick me up a cashier's check for my alimony payment."

FROM THE BACK OF THE HOUSE

"The van (JIM'S customer courtesy bus) is out of gas, back left tire is flat too."

"The vacuum sweeper is broke, need bags too. Why don't you buy a new one?"

"I need a raise, man, like I need some jingle."

"I fired Julio, stealing coffee."

"Mabel called, she's sick, won't be in."

"The 'arbage 'eisposal, she is jammed."
"The what?"
"The eisposal."

"Ice Cream man says C.O.D. or he's taking the order back."
"Take it back."

"The hod water tank is leaking."
"So, plug it."
"No, it's leaking all dover de place, no hod water."

"The ladies room toilet is plugged up, overflowing."

FROM THE BACK OF THE HOUSE

"The roof has a leak."

"The basement is flooded, sump pumps broke."

"The health department was in, got a problem with the door on the ice machine."

"Major called in, sick, who's gonna cook?"

"There's a bus just pulled in, they have seventy-five from Sunset Nursing Home, wanta have lunch on the deck, separate checks, they have Entertainment Club (buy one get one free) coupons too."

"We're out of lettuce and baked potatoes."

"The guy at table 6 wants to see you, something wrong with his wife's prime rib."

"This guys American Express card won't go through, tab is $200."

"The men's room is out of towels."

"The ladies room is out of everything."

FROM THE BACK OF THE HOUSE

"When you gonna get us new uniforms?"

"Table 7 stiffed (no tip) me."

"That lady at table 12 wants to see you, think she's hot."

"That guy at station eight used up ten bottles of Heinz steak sauce, wants to know if we have any A-1."

"We're out of tablecloths."

NUMBER NINE–chefs

At JIM'S the chefs (all males) were called cooks. A steak ordered rare, cooked that way, questioned that it was not cooked enough by the eater, brought back to the kitchen, the cook's response could be, "How'd the basteed ike dit blackened?" Cook questioned further, another response might be, "Get out of my f___ing kitchen!"

In general, chef, cook (sous or otherwise) these unique creatures are not employees, they are on loan from God and they let the manager/owner/other employees know it. Especially, when umpteen food orders are in, the house is jammed, do they let their on-loan from God status be known.

It's not a verbal let-it-be-known thing, it's body language, a squinty eye look, a mean gleam in there. However it's

FROM THE BACK OF THE HOUSE

conveyed, it's as clear as any verbal language yet found on planet earth.

In short, it says (especially when a hundred hungry customers are waiting for food in the dinning room), "If I walk out, what are you gonna do, run (the polite term is run, the other word begins with s) or go blind?"

NUMBER TEN–servers

People serving customers at eating establishments have been and are called many things. Aside from the quality of service perspective–SOB, Bitch, Bastard, Hey You, etc.–they are referred to as waitress, waiter, and more recently, since around 1970, servers.

At JIM'S (up until around the Ford Edsel) these people, all female, dressed in starched white uniforms, silk nylons, and white shoes, were called, "girls." Try that today.

Anyway, Servers:

"Why do we have to split tips?"

"If we had a microwave in the kitchen we could heat up the baked potatoes."

"Table six, just left, jerks left me a two-dollar tip."

"Guy on six wants to see you, wife's steak is not cooked

FROM THE BACK OF THE HOUSE

right."

"Guys at twelve want garlic on their steak, Major [cook] refuses to do it, wanta ya want to do?"

"Lady at the round table wants to know why you spend all your time in the lounge."

"When are we getting new uniforms?"

Please, no more. Maybe just a note in defense of servers and restaurant service in general: with the advent of fast food drive-through windows, many people have become accustomed to ordering at a speaker, paying at a window, seconds later picking up their food at another window, then as they drive away, dodge traffic, and talk on a cell phone, chow down.

Still others order at a counter, pay, wait a minute, take food to a plastic table and while reading a newspaper and/or looking at others, and/or talking on a cell phone, eat.

Is it any wonder, in a traditional restaurant where a server comes to a table, takes an order, places it with a cook, the food is being prepared (sometimes minutes are involved), people become upset, frustrated, angry, mean.

I think it's that stomach thing mentioned above. Or is it

FROM THE BACK OF THE HOUSE

something else working in the overall scheme of things, evolution of digestive juices to accommodate a higher level of expletive deleted.

Looking back to my brief experience at the JIM'S helm, a thought filters through: when you're bad in life, die, the luck-shysters put you in the restaurant business.

In any case, if some restaurant deal sounds too good to be true, be careful, you're dead a long long time and Satan calls it the hospitality business.

Anyway, back to beginnings.

3
KISS

Nothing (okay almost nothing) is chronological in the restaurant business (if chronological by chance ever happened, Ray Rockey would have caught it, floured it, fried it and put it on the menu with some kind of special chronometer sauce) so skipping back a couple hundred or so years let's go back to the beginning where it all (maybe not all, depending on your "creative design" perspective) began. At least Cleveland, the Flats, and Jim's Steak House began.

As to KISS, one time I asked a guy what that meant, KISS. He looked at me like a hawk looks at a young chicken. "Keep it simple, stupid."

So, in keeping with the best of KISS, why are the Flats called the Flats? The response from those in the know and the Flats Oxbow Association: "The Flats is the flat land on both banks of the Cuyahoga River."

Like the guy said, especially when it gets down between or below the cracks and nobody cares, KISS, try at least. So here goes.

How this brief history relates to Jim's Steak House becomes clear later.

Around two hundred plus years ago (1796) enter Moses Cleaveland* (that's how Moses spelled his last name). There are many myths about how the "a" got dropped giving us today's Cleveland. One story goes, a local "penny press"

FROM THE BACK OF THE HOUSE

typesetter (working lopsided, late for lunch, drunk, or all three) omitted, dropped or lost the typesetter's *a* and it goes from there.

In any case, Moses Cleaveland was born, January 29, 1754 in Canterbury, Connecticut. He fought in the Revolutionary War and, after the dust settled, went to Yale, graduating with a law degree, set up a law practice in Canterbury, and married Esther Champion. Soon thereafter he and she produced four children. Things moving along, Moses must have been relatively successful as a barrister because, thinking futures he got together with some locals and formed the Connecticut Land Company. Just so happens (who had whose ear at ye Olde Boar's Head Pub in Canterbury only the bar maids knew for sure) there existed in northeastern Ohio a pretty nice tract of land (around three million acres) up for sale and later to be known as the Western Reserve. Seems the land had been claimed by Connecticut in some kind of treaty deal with the Native Americans.

So, looking to expand, Moses's and Company, in 1795, bought said Western Reserve which later became part of Ohio. The total price paid, $1,200,000, came out at around "cheap" per acre. Moses's share, $32,000, makes cheap look expensive.

And so, deal in hand, the Connecticut Land Company

FROM THE BACK OF THE HOUSE

wanting to know just what they had bought, Moses formed a surveying party to go see and, April 28, 1796, the group headed west. The trip (Canterbury to Cleveland, 600 miles, driving time today, around 10 hours) would take (by horse) Moses and company a couple months. Turns out the trek would have been a reality television producer's dream come true. To wit: Moses and group, drinking stream water (they bathed in it too) roughed it through swamps, gnats, mosquitoes, and assorted wild animals. Breakfast, lunch, snacks, and dinner consisted of rabbit, squirrel, fish and plucked berries. Hygiene pretty much in the tank, no surprise many of the group came down with dysentery.

Nevertheless, as the team forged west, a hitch: running into some of the locals (Native Americans, I.e., Indians), evidently the Natives had not been tipped off as to the Connecticut land-deal treaty.

"What treaty?" said the locals.

It should be noted, in the pre-reservation years, the Indians had learned to speak English, in particular "what" followed by "treaty."

In any case, Moses being surrounded by questioning local's faces, had to convince them that Connecticut had indeed, somewhere back when, signed a treaty with other locals of the protesting locals same genetic makeup.

The Indians not buying Moses's explanation, a big "Ugh,

FROM THE BACK OF THE HOUSE

white man speak with forked tongue," in Moses's face, Moses greased the situation through by dolling out some shiny beads, minted wampum, and a few vats of corn liquor. In a nut shell, the Indians got blued, screwed and tattooed. What else is new, they always got shafted.

Anyway, as expected, the locals dazzled, bamboozled and drunk, gave Moses the green light and off he and his party went, arriving July 22, 1796 at the mouth of the Cuyahoga. Surveying the surrounds, it looked like a good place to begin and Cleveland began.

A few months later, surveying done, Moses and Company, fed up and homesick, in October of 1796, returned to Canterbury.

A few of Moses's company remained and not long after more pioneers arrived. One famous settler was Lorenzo Carter. A replica of his cabin is this day on display in the Flats' Heritage Park.

The remaining pioneers, fingers in many pies, opened business (one such business, The Carter Tavern, operated on the northwest corner of W 9th and Superior) and traded with the local Native Americans.

Getting closer to the bone of the JIM'S side of this tale, in 1819 Joel Scranton arrived in the settlement of Cleveland with a load of leather (leather in demand for shoes, whatever) and soon opened a dry goods store.

FROM THE BACK OF THE HOUSE

Not long after Joel set up shop, enter James Averell. Mr. Averell, also in the leather business, teamed up with Joel and there was born Cleveland's renowned Scranton Averell Corporation. Not long after they began buying up farm land located in what would later be called the Cleveland Flats. **

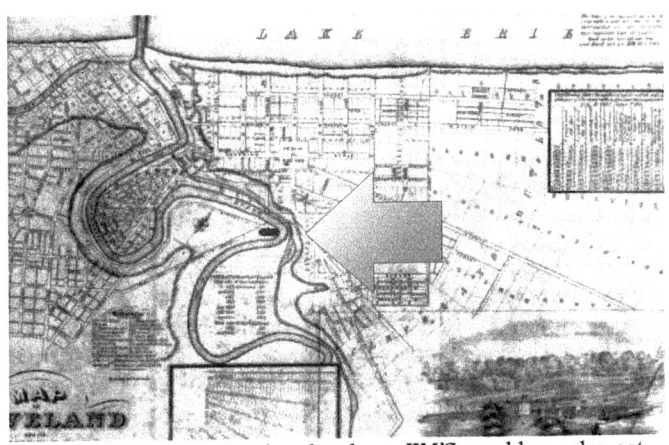

Red dot NE Scranton Peninsula where JIM'S would one day set on west bank of Cuyahoga (1835 map Ahaz Merchant)

As promised, here's where Jim's Steak House comes in: The heirs of James Averell (the Carters, no relation to Lorenzo) inherited Averell's part of the Scranton Averell Corporation. One part being a chunk of the Flats later to be known as the Scranton Peninsula and upon which, in around a hundred plus years, would set Jim's Steak House. ***

Here's where KISS people get frantic.

Around 1921 the Ratowczer (changed to Ratner of Forest

FROM THE BACK OF THE HOUSE

City fame) family emigrated to Cleveland and got into the lumber business. Some forty years later (1980s) Scranton-Averell hooked up and formed a partnership with Forest City called the Scranton Development Company.

JIM'S circa 1955

Short and simple, i.e., KISS, the whole nine yards would come back to haunt Jim's Steak House in years to come. But that's for later in the story.

---

*Moses's end date November 16, 1806, a statue by sculptor James G. C. Hamilton stands in Cleveland's Public Square.

**The Pioneer Families of Cleveland, Gertrude Wickham, Evangelical Publishing House 1914; History of Cleveland; Case Historical Society; Encyclopedia of Cleveland

***Stickney & Stickney Law Firm, Cleveland

4

GREECE, CLEVELAND & PITTSBURGH
THE FIRST JIM'S

Like someone said, or should have said, most things (okay almost most) are conceived by someone with a dream, a plan, a way to make a change. Turns out, more than not, the change equates with some commercial activity of one kind or another and dreams get linked to nickels and dimes.

Along the dream lines, a few think the Original Designer, holding all the change anyway, why all the madness? But that's getting off track.

Getting back to Jim's Steak House. In the home of Plato, Aristotle, and the gyro (that would be Greece) on August 28, 1883 a boy was born. Christened James Kerkles, the seed of Ulysses lurking in his young DNA, he matured into young manhood with the dream of distant lands and far away places fermenting in him. Fermentation ripe, at the age of twenty-two, he packed his dream in a suitcase, boarded a steam ship and, April 4 1905 landed in the land of the free, home of the brave, Capitalism, and democracy. Not necessarily in that order.

After a U.S.A. Ellis Island welcome, processing, and who are you, we're not sure what Kerkles did in the seventeen years from 1905 to 1922. One thing we do know, out beyond the Hudson River, the greening of America was taking place with the new frontier beckoning like a whiff of land to a sea weary sailor.

One location beckoning Kerkles was bugled off the lips of saloon keepers and newspaper editors as the golden capital of the new boon, bust, and me-too. The location–Cleveland, Ohio.

No surprise, Kerkles joined the stampede west and by train, boat, horse or all three, at the age of 39, arrived in Cleveland where archives record his naturalization: *

Kerkles James
Address: 1149 W. 9th Street, Cleveland, Ohio
2288445 - Vo. 84, pg. 159 Court of Common Pleas, Cuyahoga County, Cleveland, Ohio
Born: Greece Aug. 28, 1883
Date and Port: April 4, 1905, New York
Naturalized: 1-Apr-26
Witnesses: John M. Sulzmann, 1338 E. 81st Street and John D. Rodgers, Parma, Ohio

The Kerkles story unfolding, he settled into an apartment

NO. 1147 W. 9TH STREET—Registration rolls show

FROM THE BACK OF THE HOUSE

at 1147 W. 9th Street.

Living here he landed a job at one of Cleveland's emerging downtown hotels. After some time learning the hospitality trade, that universal me-too fire glowing hot in him, he saw a need to better feed, succor, and otherwise comfort weary travelers. The need he saw confirmed in his daily hotel choirs, he made one of those once-in-a-lifetime moves that alters the course of human events. Families at least–Kerkles opened a small eatery and called it, what else, RESTAURANT.

The eatery, catering to (displayed on the front window) "Ladies and Gentlemen," also served lumbermen, traveling salesmen, sailors, railroad workers, and the general Cleveland lunch bunch.

Kerkles in front of his restaurant

FROM THE BACK OF THE HOUSE

And so began what would become Cleveland's much loved (later moved to a new location) Jim's Steak House.

More profoundly, the JIM'S clan saga was about to begin and many family's (Rockey, Mercurio, Ferra, Marsico) genealogy scrapbooks would be changed forever.

---
*<http://www.rootsweb.com/~ohcuyah2/nats/coarch/part3/pg0121.html>

5
HILDA

The JIM'S family saga bloomed when, into James' restaurant strolled a rare (some say exceptional) find from

Ms. Hilda Hoffman

Pittsburgh Pennsylvania–twenty-four year old Hilda Theresa Hoffman.

How Hilda got from Pittsburgh to Cleveland we don't know or some are not telling. One rumor has it that Hilda ran away

FROM THE BACK OF THE HOUSE

from home. Whatever, a Hollywood scenario might go like this:

Hilda hops a bus to Cleveland; arrived, she goes into James Kerkles' RESTAURANT for a cup of coffee, piece of apple pie. James, short of help, waiting on customers, Hilda drops her fork and James makes his move.

Those familiar with Hilda suggest it might have been the other way 'round. In any event, Cuyahoga County probate court records show, September 12, 1923, James 38, and Hilda 24, tied the knot. The record lists Hilda's occupation as nurse. The nurse notation a fantasy (her mother and sister were nurses) maybe she needed to look not kidnaped.

You decide.

FROM THE BACK OF THE HOUSE

Anyway, nuptial bliss secured, the newlyweds took up house keeping in Kerkles' apartment at 1149 W. 9th and in short order Hilda began assisting James with his dream RESTAURANT.

A typical menu reveals specials of the day:

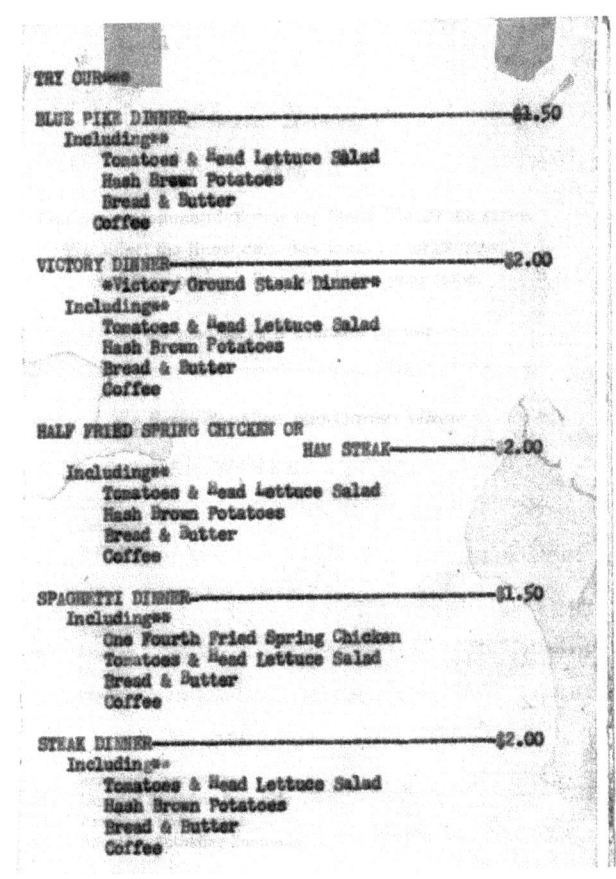

TRY OUR

BLUE PIKE DINNER————————————$1.50
   Including:
      Tomatoes & Head Lettuce Salad
      Hash Brown Potatoes
      Bread & Butter
      Coffee

VICTORY DINNER————————————$2.00
   "Victory Ground Steak Dinner"
   Including:
      Tomatoes & Head Lettuce Salad
      Hash Brown Potatoes
      Bread & Butter
      Coffee

HALF FRIED SPRING CHICKEN OR
                    HAM STEAK————$2.00
   Including:
      Tomatoes & Head Lettuce Salad
      Hash Brown Potatoes
      Bread & Butter
      Coffee

SPAGHETTI DINNER————————————$1.50
   Including:
      One Fourth Fried Spring Chicken
      Tomatoes & Head Lettuce Salad
      Bread & Butter
      Coffee

STEAK DINNER————————————$2.00
   Including:
      Tomatoes & Head Lettuce Salad
      Hash Brown Potatoes
      Bread & Butter
      Coffee

FROM THE BACK OF THE HOUSE

Among the Blue Pike, Ground Steak, Spring Chicken, and Spaghetti Dinners, as an added special for Kerkles, Hilda washed floors, walls, and dishes while he managed. As in the dropped fork business with Hilda (some who know swear) "managed" was in Kerkles' mind only.

One thing not in Kerkles' "mind only" was Prohibition. In effect (January 16, 1920, repealed in 1933) if he poured a shot and a beer at his joint it was under the table or in a back room. Bet on the back room.

Regarding prohibition, before the law went into effect, Cleveland had twelve thousand legal bars. A year after the tea teetotalers' law went into effect, there were an estimated three thousand illegal speakeasies. Not only that, there were an estimated 40,000 bootleggers (not all in the mafia) around town selling liquor to a hundred thousand thirsty citizens. Topping it off, the report suggests nine out of ten prohibition enforcement officers (some rumor the list included Elliot of Ness fame) were on somebody's payroll besides the taxpayers. (The Encyclopedia of Cleveland History)

Long and short of it, Prohibition didn't work. Why is this not a surprise? It's why a Higher Authority came up with a unique idea called *free will.* Legislating morality never works, just like it's not working now. The only people who made any money back then were Al Capone types and a few enforcement officers. Ditto these days for contemporary drug

FROM THE BACK OF THE HOUSE

dealers. But you could get in trouble going there or dead.

Anyway, we have to assume that Kerkles offered a little hooch under the table or the place was dry. Bet on the first.

Meanwhile, Kerkles' RESTAURANT (now with Hilda) not only humming but singing along, adding insult to illegal hooch, October 29, 1929 the stock market crashed. Some scholars speculate the crash was all brought on by Prohibition. The reasoning: those gents on Wall Street, accustomed to a leisurely three-martini-lunch, were forced to imbibe their gin from (instead of a stemmed glass) a coffee mug behind a back room door. The whole thing messed up their figuring.

The depression lasting until 1939, bottomed out around the same time the Prohibition boondoggle ended Dec 5, 1933. The market's upswing begun in '33, scholars further suggest the booze repeal, coupled with the same year market lift, proved their theory–the market rise was no coincidence. A few insist it's ninety scientific proof that booze boosts the economy.

In any case, in competition with bootleggers, soup kitchens, and the Salvation Army, team Kerkles and Hilda kept their restaurant open through it all.

Jim's STEAK HOUSE

6
LUMBER MEETS STEER STEAK

Kerkles' RESTAURANT fast becoming a favorite Cleveland eating and beverage spot, came another fork in that famous road. Where these forks occur has frustrated philosophers through the ages. The Greeks blamed three ladies weaving thread. Lottery winners call it luck. Still others profess it's all the doings of a higher authority, not to be understood let alone thought about by mere mortals.

Whatever the spin, in the early 1900's much of the Cleveland Flats might have been considered, with lumber yards everywhere, a lumberman's Disney Land.

Especially so, with stacks of lumber four stories high, was the Scranton Peninsula at Collision Bend.

Collision Bend circa 1930 (Cleveland Then and Now, Grabowski & Grabowski)

FROM THE BACK OF THE HOUSE

It comes as no surprise, amid all that lumber fantasy, Cleveland's lumber barons desired a place near their lumber to talk, smoke, shmooze, and dine with fellow barons. So, desire being what it is, the barons either owned (landlord of record not found, goes back to the previously mentioned Joel Scranton, James Averell connection, owning the Scranton Peninsula land) bought, built, or leased a three-story brick building located (in a place later to be called the Flats) at 1782 Scranton Road. The baron's new club house was just south of a swing bridge (removed with the 1940 widening of Collision Bend) that crossed the Cuyahoga River a-little north of Carter Road.

View from Terminal Tower prior to widening of Collision Bend

The three-story brick building (in circle), new home to the

FROM THE BACK OF THE HOUSE

Lumbermen's Club, became the center of the Cleveland lumber baron's social activities.

The Cleveland Press (March 8, 1939) put it this way: "Pulling up in fancy buggies, lashing steeds to hitching posts in front of the club were the carriages of the famous titans of the Cleveland lumber business. The chieftains' wives decked out in hoop dresses, they dined, partied, and danced by the light of crackling pine fires."

Alas, while the lumber chieftains partied by the light of crackling fire, the fate weavers (some say luck-shysters) were scheming overtime.

To wit: Across the Cuyahoga and just up the street from the lumbermen's clubhouse, the Terminal Tower and Public Square (years in the completing) project was finished in 1931. The Terminal Tower being the tallest building east of New York and west of Chicago, record keepers heralded the tower BIG DADDY.

No surprise, with that kind of national recognition, Cleveland's Public Square became the local muckety-muck place to hobnob, be seen, rub elbows and what not. Hobnob and elbow rubbing being what it is, we have to assume places-to-be-seen must have been on the lumber baron's minds. More probably on the baron's wives' minds, the lumber boys decided to move their club up the hill to the new plum location smack dab in the shadow of BIG DADDY.

FROM THE BACK OF THE HOUSE

Fate's plot thickening, news seeped out that the old Lumbermen's Club building, soon to be vacated, a tenant might ought apply. Say no more. James Kerkles caught wind of the news and, that seed of Ulysses sparking his DNA, events might have gone like this:

Images of a big time eatery filling Kerkles' thoughts, he rushes in the back door of his RESTAURANT's kitchen where Hilda is flipping a steak.

Kerkles to Hilda: "Honey bun, you're not gonna believe it, too good to be true, a one-in-a-lifetime opportunity . . ."

Hilda: "Some jerk walked out on a three dollar tab at lunch."

Kerkles: ". . .the Lumbermen's Club, ya know, down in the Flats, that four story brick building, right on the Cuyahoga river, living quarters upstairs, dining facilities on the first floor . . .."

Hilda: "You need ta order a peck of potatoes and . . . "

Kerkles: " . . . the lumbermen are moving their club up town . . . Vacating their club house, that building was made for us!"

Imagination aside, Kerkles rushed out to seize fate by the throat, did, and shortly thereafter, a deal was struck * and he and Hilda (around 1931) moved into the˙ Lumbermen's Club building. Living upstairs, restaurateuring downstairs, life was good.

FROM THE BACK OF THE HOUSE

In an early snapshot of the building the sign painted on

the side reads JIM'S PLACE. In a later Cleveland Press photo a sign over the door reads Jim's Steak House.

About the name, it's been said an inside squabble between Hilda and James over naming of the new joint, whatever was said between the sheets, we now know Hilda was pitching Jim's Steak House.

By the way, the painted billboard on the left side of the building reads: STEER STEAK DINNERS FAMOUS FROM COAST TO COAST

Anyway, naming rights settled, two years after moving in, prohibition repealed, liquor back on the top shelf, JIM'S

FROM THE BACK OF THE HOUSE

offered 30 cent shots of *Old Calvert*.

The new JIM'S location fast became a hot spot for Clevelanders, with people from far and wide stopping in for a steak, hash brown potatoes, and a good shot of whiskey.

One special bunch that found safe haven at JIM'S was sailors and captains from the Great Lakes shipping freighters.

Julina Griffin of the Cleveland Press put it this way:

> Time was when she [Aunt Hilda] knew virtually all the lakes skippers by name. That was when the bridges remained closed to river traffic during the morning and afternoon rush hours, forcing the boats to tie up for an hour or two and the sailing people went over the side to have themselves a snort and a steak . . .
>
> Today skippers still visit her when in port

FROM THE BACK OF THE HOUSE

and in winter when their ships are laid up. Shipping executives with offices in downtown Cleveland frequently drop down the hill and across the bridge for lunch or dinner. (Cleveland Press, Ship&Shore, May 5, 1952)

Joining the sailors were meat and potato epicure seeking executive big shots from a hundred Flats' mills and factories.

Meantime, JIM'S business booming, back in Hilda's hometown of Pittsburgh, Pennsylvania things were brewing that would have down-the-road consequences for the Jim's Steak House clan forever thereafter.

---

*As noted above, the Carters owned the land way back to the Scranton Averell connection. Who owned the building is beyond the scope of this memoir, most probably the lumbermen. When the building was to be later demolished for the widening of Collision Bend, there was no mention of moving it.

7

TRUTH OR PITTSBURGH CONSEQUENCES

Aunt Hilda had four siblings–sisters Lena, Mary, Elsie and a brother, Joseph. Of interest to this stroll down memory lane is Hilda's sister, Mary. Betrothed to Pittsburgh Jeweler, Charley Rockey, Mary gave birth, February 4, 1924, to a son, Raymond. As noted at the outset, for those familiar with Jim's Steak House, flash bulbs might be going off along with bells and sirens. For those not familiar, Mary and Charley Rockey's son was none other than the future manager and owner (to be known in later years around Cleveland as the Flats' notorious restauranteur) of Jim's Steak House, Raymond Charles Rockey.

Digging deeper into this memory-lane stroll, turns out young Raymond's favorite Uncle was Aunt Hilda's husband, James Kerkles. Raymond is reported to have been "happily excited" when he heard Uncle Jim and Aunt Hilda were coming to Pittsburgh. When Jim and Hilda were not traveling to Pittsburgh, Raymond wangled, begged or finagled a ride to Ohio so he could be with the revered Cleveland restaurant duo.

Still deeper in clan lore, just when everybody thought they had it all figured out, fate did it again: Mary and Charley's marriage on the rocks, Raymond's mother, Mary, died. Charley quicky remarried and you have the beginning of a soap opera, at least a Nora Robert's novel.

FROM THE BACK OF THE HOUSE

In any case, Charley hitched again, for whatever reason Raymond ended up with his mother Mary's parents in Pittsburgh. Fate weavers on ninety proof something, becoming erratic, there erupted months of legal battles, between Raymond's father and his mother's side of the family, over custody of young Raymond. On his mother's side, Aunt Hilda, true to form in the front, back, and middle of the fray, guess what? She won. Raymond moved permanently to Cleveland to live with her and James. Then and forever (James and Hilda no children of there own) Raymond became Aunt Hilda's "my boy."

Young Raymond removed from the Pittsburgh strife, basking in the glow of only child son-ship, lived a boy's dream adventure in the old four story Lumbermen's club, now home to Jim's Steak House. One

Raymond

FROM THE BACK OF THE HOUSE

can only imagine the nooks and crannies in the ancient building he explored, things he found.

We do know one thing found him–Rats! Ray often told the story: "Late one night in bed I felt something moving on top of the covers. I peeked to see what it was and found a rat crawling on the bedspread." He recalled deftly swooping the spread around the beast and tossing, bedspread and all, out a nearby open window.

Over the years, along with furry friends, the smell of Flats' soot and grease, the acrid Cuyahoga oozing a few feet away, oar boats blasting their horns in the night, grilling sirloin, frying hash browns, fat rendering, and the aroma of beer and ale, Raymond became Aunt Hilda's Tom Sawyer, Huckleberry Finn, and Peck's Bad Boy hermetically sealed all in one.

Sneaking a nip behind the bar, snapping perfumed bras of the JIM'S "girls," playing ladies' room peek-a-boo, inhaling cigarette and cigar smoke (some his own), and frequent pecks from cooing JIM'S lady customers, a unique restaurant kind of DNA seeped into his being and he morphed into a unique rascal. Some think Aunt Hilda loved, even promoted, his roguishness. If she didn't approve of the behavior, it didn't work.

Growing up in the limelight, young Raymond minced shenanigan time between academics at Benedictine High School and the JIM'S kitchen where he fast became a skilled

FROM THE BACK OF THE HOUSE

sculler.

Sculler. That's a nice term for one who does what Army sergeants call grunt work, kitchen patrol, K.P. In short, washing dishes, scouring pots, cleaning grease traps, mopping floors, scrubbing toilets and whatever else is assigned or nobody volunteers for.

Almost before "my boy" knew it, like a young tomato plant fed Miracle Grow, he bloomed. And in it all, he did what anybody would do, he fell in love with the hype and "restaurant center-stage" way of life.

In later years, brandishing his Tom and Huck image, Ray liked to go "up town" to fancy Cleveland restaurants dressed in his faded blue jeans, well-worn loafers, and stained white T-shirt. Most hosts, owners, hostesses knew him, let him pass. To the ones who didn't he'd just say, "Ray Rockey, Jim's Steak House," and whisk by. Other times, on odd hour visits to *the* Steak House when the restaurant was closed, the sign in the front window displaying OPEN, reminded of the sign, he would say, "I know, keeps 'em guessing."

But before the later years, the fate weavers at it again in Hilda and young Raymond's life, another shoe dropped.

8

DEKINKING

In 1938, the Terminal Tower pretty much Cleveland's

Navigating Collision Bend prior to widening (Cleveland Memory Project, Cleveland State University)

skyline, things at the new JIM'S location going along swimmingly, what usually happens when things are moving along swimmingly, around March of '38, the fate spinners became restless and up popped another "fork" in the clan's road.

Why this particular "fork" popped up at this particular time is (as it commonly is) a matter of commerce. To wit: Cuyahoga River traffic increasing, the oar boats getting longer and bigger, navigating the "crooked river" had become a "bump in the nightmare." Especially nasty, was that tight squeeze around Collision Bends which, even with a tug at

FROM THE BACK OF THE HOUSE

bow and stern, had many a skipper reaching for a bottle of Johnny Walker Black.

So, responding to the mounting gripes from skippers and ship owners, the U.S. Corps of Engineers, City Planers or both, decided they had to do something and, eminent domain being what it is, guess what?

While you're guessing, one wonders how, when the final chapter on earthly matters is closed, the Higher Ups will handle the matter of eminent domain.

In any event, just eight years after James and Hilda moved their restaurant and home (and now with young Raymond in tow) into the Lumbermen's Club, earthly powers announced grand plans for the 'dekinking' of fabled Collision Bend:

The Cleveland Press story below the photo, Wednesday, March 8, 1939 says it in one punch:

James Kerkles in insert

FROM THE BACK OF THE HOUSE

The Press story:

> Steam shovels at Collision Bend today gnawed their way toward the old Lumbermen's Club in the Flats . . . The four-story landmark, at 1782 Scranton Road in the shadow of the Terminal Tower, is doomed for destruction within the next 18 months because the Cuyahoga River is having its kinks snipped, and the building lies squarely in the way . . .
>
> Kerkles and his wife, Hilda, said they would keep on running the restaurant for the next 18 months, or until the very moment that the steam shovels on the river-dekinking project move right up to the restaurant door.
>
> Kerkle and his wife have operated a restaurant in the building for eight years. Mrs. Kerkles estimated today that during this period they have served 280,000 steaks.
>
> As Kerkles watched the pile drivers pound sheets of steel bulk heading along the river's new shore line, he said: "It's not right for me to move. I've had people in from all over the world. I'm doing more business now than ever before."

Shouting out loud, what else is new? The higher-ups won again and fate's fat cousin threw James Kerkles a big craps. Just four months after the newspaper article chronicled "doomed destruction within 18 months" James Kerkles, June 15, 1939, not in good health anyway (he had diabetes), age 56, missed the Good Book's promised "three score and ten" by 14 years.

FROM THE BACK OF THE HOUSE

James eulogized, funeral over, one can only imagine what hobgoblins tramped around in the mind of forty year old Hilda. Think about it. Deference to Thomas Paine, not only was this the time that tired souls, she doubted if souls even existed. What's more, between doubts she had to wonder if God, while playing monopoly with Louie, arguing with the bad boy about what went wrong with the Adam and Eve plot, played fiddle in the meantime.

The why of it all nagging at her sanity, cringing at each steam shovel's gnawing grab into the banks of the Cuyahoga, Hilda remained dauntless. Will of steel, huddling "my boy" close, she would protect her Raymond and keep her first loves' dream alive.

9
WATER LINE BREAK!

A husband just buried, JIM'S still open for business, Hilda not only needed to find a new home for JIM'S, she had to have a place for herself and "my boy" to sleep. At this point many people would have thrown in the towel. But Hilda, with a skillet in one hand and broom in the other, didn't blink as she eyed (some 120 feet away from her soon to be demolished building) a plot of land that would escape the dekinking shovels of the Corps of Engineers.

Luck, fate, whatever, it just so happened the Carters (James Averell heirs) owned the land she eyed. Voila the word for the day, Hilda contacted the Carters, told them of her

Even after the new JIM'S home is completed (bottom center) there is still a lot of Flats' dirt around

FROM THE BACK OF THE HOUSE

plight (they probably already knew) and discussed the piece of their unkinkable land for construction of a new JIM'S.

A gas station at the corner of Scranton and Carter operated by CLEVE-CO would not be a problem. Hilda wanted the land behind the station.

Corner Scranton and Carter Road, circa 1940 (Cleveland Memory Project, Cleveland State University)

The Carter's response, "What's to lose, nothing there but Flats dirt, weeds, and factory dust, we can work it out."

And so, amid toasts, steak dinner, and drinks the parties of the first, second, and umpteenth parts agreed (for whatever reason the land was not for sale at the time, or the cost beyond Hilda's grasp) and Hilda signed a multiple year land lease with the Carters.

FROM THE BACK OF THE HOUSE

The ink not yet dry, building plans for a new JIM'S scribbled on the end of a tablecloth, Hilda taxied (she didn't drive) to her uptown banker. Applying for a construction loan, Hilda was asked by the bank manager what she had for collateral. Her reply, "What the hell is collateral?"

She must have made an impression because the loan was approved. So, still operating her restaurant out of the doomed Lumbermen's Club building, the dekinking of the Cuyahoga moving closer each day, Hilda now needed a contractor to begin construction of a new JIM'S home.

Between 'finger walking" the yellow pages, pealing potatoes, and seating the JIM'S lunch crowd, she glanced out a window to check on the Corps of Engineer's dekinking progress. A second glance confirmed, there he stood, five foot six, the co-owner of The Standard Excavating Company, Frank Paul Mercurio Sr.* Smiling like he knew who crafted the Rosetta stone, the big paesanos grin was to Hilda like a lighthouse beacon in the night.

Frank's charm magnetic, next thing you know he's inside JIM'S having coffee with Hilda. A little this, a that, turns out The Standard Excavating Company had been contracted to work on the dekinking of the Cuyahoga.

A little more a this, a lot a that, and right out of a Frank Capra movie, Frank was hired to proceed with the construction of Hilda's new Jim's Steak House.

FROM THE BACK OF THE HOUSE

A few weeks later, shovel in hand, Hilda broke ground and more than one foundation was begun.

FROM THE BACK OF THE HOUSE

To cement it all in Flats' dirt, they took a group photo.

Look close, third from the left stands Frank. Wearing a hat from Godfather Inc., tweaking his index finger, he seems to be smiling like he just got a free case of extra virgin olive oil from cousin Luigi in Palermo.

Turns out the smile, when construction got off to a rocky start, was short lived. Juliana Griffin of the Cleveland Press recounts (from a Hilda interview) the incident blow by blow:

> She [Hilda] had to move the palace 125 feet back because of the river straightening program. Otherwise, she would now be in the

middle of the Cuyahoga. She hired Frank Mercurio, a contractor in the dekinking, who operates Standard Excavating Co., to dig the new foundation. In probing around on Saturday his men broke a water main and shut off her supply [of water].

That did it. Hilda, still operating JIM's out of the Lumbermen's Club (she and Raymond living upstairs), blew a gasket. Juliana's article continued:

> She [Hilda] raised the roof. The first thing Monday she went to her lawyer and filed suit for damages. (Cleveland Press, May 5, 1952)

Bottom line, Hilda sued Frank, Standard Excavating Company, and all the white horses they rode in on. And, as usual, she won the battle.

But trumping the win, in true son-of-the-boot style, a few years hence, when recalling the incident, Frank would declare, "But I won the war." More later.

Anyway, after Hilda sued, won, the Flat's dust settled, only the muses know for sure what rolled off the silver tongue of goombah Frank. Whatever he pitched, Hilda must have listened because he continued the job.

And so, back about 125 feet from the Cuyahoga River's old channel, out of reach of the "dekinking," construction was completed for the new home of Jim's Steak House, with living

FROM THE BACK OF THE HOUSE

quarters, for Hilda and "my boy" Raymond, above.

---

*Frank's partner in Standard was Frank Monniti. Among other things the two Franks dug holes around Cleveland, owned dump trucks, bulldozers, steam shovels, lunched with the crowd on Murray Hill. In later years, The Cleveland Press, December 3, 1953, reported:"$32,000 spent in Celebrezze race for mayor . . . bigger contributors included $250.00 from Frank Mercurio and Frank Monniti . . ."

10

NEW HOME, ROMANCE AND RIVALRY

This photo dated June1941 shows the Collision Bend

project well under way and JIM'S (arrow) in its new digs. The old Lumbermen's Club building long gone, a good chunk of the Scranton Peninsular becoming history, Scranton Road is dead ended. The Flats' Fire Station #21 is moved back to a space close to the bottom of the Eagle Street ramp bridge. Note that the Jim's Steak House stone-in-grass sign was laid out on the front lawn by (on her knees) who else, Hilda T.

FROM THE BACK OF THE HOUSE

Things settled down a bit for Hilda, with "my boy" and JIM'S in their new home, Frank Mercurio had also found a new hangout.

To wit, what is it they say, Germans and Italians naturally get along. They say a lot of things. Some sayings become fact, get written down in books. That says it all.

In any case, Frank's Italian DNA dating back to B.C., and Hilda, of good German stock, the German/Italian myth stuck. They not only got along, a romance heated up.

Related to that, a matter not much discussed in the back of the house, not even on top of the house, was Frank's marital status. In the best omerta (Sicilian- keep your mouth shut) he remained married, separated, divorce in the works,

FROM THE BACK OF THE HOUSE

or all three.

We do know (at some point in time) Frank was married and had at least one son, Frank Jr., who worked for Frank Sr. at Standard Excavating. We know this because of a much clan talked about cup-throwing incident between the two Franks to be detailed later.

Be that as it may, marriage not currently in the cards, Hilda (minus first-love James) keeping an ever watchful eye on *The* Steak House till, now had two boys in her world, both vying for her attention: Frank, busy digging-holes all over Cleveland, enjoying a new place to lunch; and "my boy" Raymond, fingers in many pies, sculling in the heat of JIM's kitchen.

Hilda, Raymond, and Jim's Steak House new home (and Frank's hangout)

11
INKLING, ANKLEING & ANCHORS AWAY

Hilda, this side of being without first husband love (James) catering to her second husband's (Frank) epicure needs, Raymond (now in the shadow of the new paesano on the block) noticed his lion share of affection slipping away.

Vestiges of abandonment lurked somewhere only God and Freud followers know, to make up for the slippage, "my boy" showered Hilda with hugs, kisses, and beyond-the-call sculling in the JIM'S kitchen. Alas, as in tales, yarns and Wall Mart romance novels, hand-on-the-tiller Frank smiled all the way to the dinner table and beyond.

In the meantime Raymond along with high school pal Tony Liotta (Tony would later become JIM'S assistant

Ray

Tony

manager, date one of Ray's ex wive, be fired . . . to be continued), graduated from Benedictine High in the spring of 1941.

High school diploma in hand, Frank mucking up his life,

FROM THE BACK OF THE HOUSE

hatayagonnado Raymond contemplated futures. Some say he had an inkling for serving people food and drink. Still others think the inkling had more to do with ankleing, as in JIM'S "girls." Whatever, Frank's hand on the tiller being what it was, amid "my boy's" contemplations, six or so months after graduation, December 7, 1941, Japan upped the contemplating ante.

The Selective Service Draft in full swing, male oedipal juices conflicting, Raymond now the second banana of Hilda's eye, joined the U.S. Coast Guard.

Reporting for duty December 1942, he began submarine training then went on to radar school (he would later tell throbbing genteel hearts not to worry, the radar has zapped his sterling) and served on the U.S.S. Mayflower, S.S. Youngstown, several others.

Radaring around the seas, dropping DNA at assorted ports (Buffalo, Norfolk, Duluth, Grand Haven and more),one of those dear-john letters showed up at mail call. Ray, opening the letter, excitement (nobody knows for sure but you have to bet) turned to four letter words.

FROM THE BACK OF THE HOUSE

Why?

Seems Tootsie and Frank were tying the knot. My boy, probably after a short trip topside for a heady heave, requested leave, returned to Cleveland, witnessed the event, and posed with the happy couple on *the* Steak House lawn.

Ray, back row, second from left

FROM THE BACK OF THE HOUSE

The wedding over, Raymond back on board ship, near the end of his enlistment wrote two letters to Aunt Hilda that lend some insight into Raymond's state of mind. The letter envelope (eight cent airmail) is addressed to Mrs. Hilda T. Kerkles.

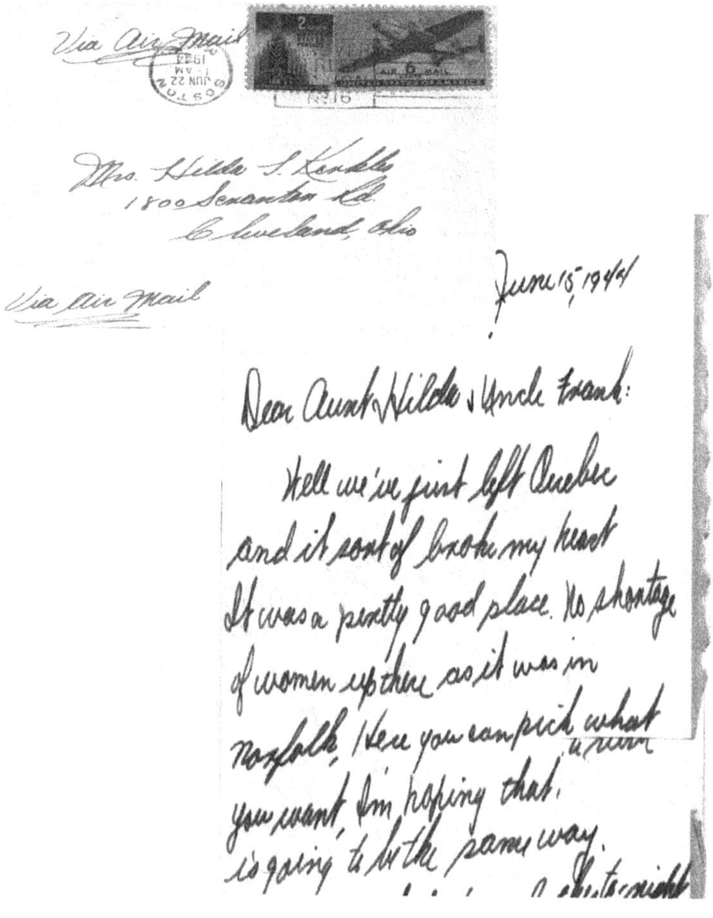

[handwritten envelope and letter, dated June 15, 1944, addressed to Mrs. Hilda J. Kerkles, 1800 Scranton Rd., Cleveland, Ohio]

Dear Aunt Hilda & Uncle Frank:

Well we've just left Quebec and it sort of broke my heart. It was a pretty good place. No shortage of women up there as it was in Norfolk. Here you can pick what you want. I'm hoping that is going to be the same way...

FROM THE BACK OF THE HOUSE

The inside salutation (shrinks, bone readers, and masseuses beware of over interpretation) is addressed to both Hilda and Frank.

The letter, spelling and punctuation faithfully reproduced, Raymond writes home:

June 15, 1944 Dear Aunt Hilda & Uncle Frank: Well we've just left Quebec and it sort of broke my heart It was a pretty good place. No shortage of women up there as it was in Norfolk, Here you can pick what you want, I'm hoping that [word or words cut out in original letter, possibly by Naval Censor] *could be Boston since letter six days later confirms arrival there] is going to be the same way.*

Have washed a few clothes tonight. Whites for the galley. I sent those others to [looks like Mary] to wash and I have paretically a new pair but I don't want to ruin them in the [galley?]. Only 15 more days and I'll be out of it. Thank heavens for that. Well tomorrow Sigy [letter six days later refers to a bartender replacement at JIM'S] *leaves for the army. I hope you've got someone already.*

I've run out of cigarettes so

2

now so I won't have to smoke those Canadian weeds I'm smoking my pipe.

It is a miserable night to-night Rainy & cold. This damp weather causes sinus to clog up again.

Well it's lights out now in five minutes so I'll have to rush through this.

We've got a washing machine on board. An old [brand name not legible] but the trouble comes when you got to carry your water back & forth.

While we were in Montreal we didn't get no liberty because

FROM THE BACK OF THE HOUSE

of zoot suites. So just about everyone was complaining. That's a pretty good town they say.
Well folks I guess I'll close for now so until later
        Love&Kisses
           Ray

A second letter, six days later, envelope again addressed to Hilda, salutation to both:

        June 21, 1944
Dear Aunt Hilda & Uncle Frank
  Got mail yesterday but no letter from you. I got the laundry O.K.
  We got into Boston yesterday afternoon and all is well now. We had a little scare coming down from Halifax. We were half way to Boston when we got report of five subs in those water. The ship that was escorting us claimed to have picked them up a couple times. That was really a sleepless night. Five times we had general quarters that's one night I was wishing that I was home in my own bed.
  We haven't been doing much of anything now. I'm still working in the gally only 25 more meals left.
  I got paid to-day. They gave me $40.00 I've got to start saving a little now because we're expecting a leave from
        2
Curtis Bay. Ten days. That wouldn't be too bad. Nice leave in summer. We keep on hoping so anyway.
  We'll be leaving for New York either to-morrow or the day after. It doesn't make any difference just so we get to Curtis Bay.
  It is really miserable weather here. Foggy and drizzling. I guess by the time I get home I'll be completely white again
  This [not legible, liaston or baston, could be Boston] *is*

FROM THE BACK OF THE HOUSE

really a lively town plenty of women and everything else. But the people here aren't as nice as some places. But I guess people in town's like these where there are plenty of service men people get tired of them.

They just brought the mail in and I got your letter of the 19th. Pretty fast service. And I'm glad that you got a bartender. I sure hope he's O.K. and that after a while you can trust him so that you'll be able to enjoy that county home. [*]

Got plenty of letters yesterday about twenty of them. Now I'll be kept busy

3

for a couple of days answering them. It's [not legible, could be pretty] *hard waiting because of not doing anything but* [not legible, could be working] *on this tub.*

It was [plenty or pretty] *rough on the way down but I didn't get sea sick. I guess my stomach wasn't in such good condition coming across Lake Superior.*

Yesterday we had to scrub down the mess hall again. Honestly its funny the paint isn't all off. On the deck the blue paint is all worn off from scrubbing. Its got the shipyard yellow showing.

Well we were just screwed out of three dollars. We gave two dollars to the Red Cross but that's a pretty good thing. But when they came around and ask 1.00 to buy a washing machine. That's pretty bad when we have to buy our own washing machine. What do you think.

Well folks I guess this letter should take

4

take [new page, take repeated] *care of the days I missed but even if the letters are fewer you know that I'm always thinking of you folks.*

Well the latest rumor is that we are going to the West Coast.

FROM THE BACK OF THE HOUSE

I don't know where they all start from but they really get around quick.
    Well folks I guess this is all for now so until later
              Love & Kisses
                    Ray

---

*"enjoy that county home" refers to the fact that Frank and Hilda (moved out of the apartment above the Steak House) had bought a house and now lived on Pleasant Valley Road from which Hilda continued (Frank drove her to work) to ramrod JIM'S.

12
Ray Rockey Returns

Raymond discharged in August 1945, he returned to visit relatives in Pittsburgh. After a day or so of dinner and up side kisses, he blew into Cleveland to say hello to the only mother he knew, Aunt Hilda. We assume he said hello to Uncle Frank too.

Writing a story in later years, Bob Seltzer, in a Cleveland Press piece wrote: "After separating from the Navy, he [Ray] contemplated more schooling under the G.I. Bill. While deliberating his course, he stopped at Jim's Steak House to help Mrs. Jim for two weeks . . ."
(Cleveland Press, November 19, 1968)

For those who know, the rest is history. For those who don't, "contemplating more schooling" was like a high school dropout contemplating being an astronaut. KISS again.

To wit: a paycheck in the hand is better than two in the contemplating. Think about it. At "my boy's" fingertips was a thriving meat and potatoes' restaurant and well-stocked bar. Icing on the cake, Hilda and Frank were now domiciled out in that country home in the Pleasant Valley boondocks.

FROM THE BACK OF THE HOUSE

Raymond had sole bedding rights to the three bedroom, two bath, fully furnished, all utilities paid, apartment above JIM'S. Free rent, free booze, free food, and the cherry on top–an unlimited assortment of "ankle desserts" running around all over the place. Heavens to Betsy!

Bottom line, Raymond's restaurant experience (that sculling thing again) along with "my boy" status payed off. Aunt Hilda put him to work full time. He did everything and then some with a paycheck to boot!

So, JIM'S humming along–Aunt Hilda well on her way to becoming the Queen of the Flats, hand-on-the-tiller Frank digging holes all around town–Raymond made notes, checked things twice, and filled among other things, his address book with more than T-bones.

As it turns out, fate and "helping out Mrs. Jim" dovetailed with Ray's post Coast Guard contemplating slicker than slicks' upper lip. The proof: a year after starting work at JIM'S (1946), at the tender age of 23, Hilda named "my boy" manager of Jim's Steak House.

Overnight, falling in that famous stink hole had new meaning. Raymond had not only dropped into that proverbial abyss, he had come out miles beyond the sweet smell of a thousand roses. In short, now manager of a booming steak house, cash register at his fingertips, nice salary plus perks, pecks, picks, food, booze, that too, not to mentioned all those

FROM THE BACK OF THE HOUSE

JIM'S "girls," life for Raymond had become shoot the moon.

23 year old JIM'S manager Ray behind JIM'S bar

And everybody said, "Let the parties begin!"

And they did, with after-hour shebangs (for select employees, pals, and friends) thrown from the roof of JIM'S to the basement. One reveler commented, "They [parties] made a Roxy (former and famous Cleveland burlesque theater on East 9th Street) performance look like a Mickey Mouse Club's roll call."

FROM THE BACK OF THE HOUSE

Parties held in Jim's basement

As to Raymond's good fate, comes to mind Rick Warren's *The Purpose Driven Life,* what Warren (some sixty years later) would write about. To wit: Raymond, in a flash of insight some never fathom, must have known beyond a doubt that this restaurant thing was what he was put on earth to do.

Slightly off track but one wonders, Mr. Warren's thesis in

FROM THE BACK OF THE HOUSE

tow, what purpose was long ago chiseled in fate for the Toms, Dicks, and Sues who sleep, eat garbage, swat flies, and die on city streets.

Anyway, next chapter.

13
The Clan's Jewel

1947 coming to a close, telephone technology once removed from two tin cans and a string, the number at JIM'S was Cherry 8787. Nestled down there on the Flat banks of the Cuyahoga, in the shadow of the Terminal Tower, the view of passing oar boats and downtown Cleveland's skyline was one of a kind.

Despite chest high windows cramping the view of the skyline (Hilda and company would be hearing about the

FROM THE BACK OF THE HOUSE

cramping from Cleveland Press food critic, Winsor French*),*the* Steak House was fast becoming the Cleveland place for booze, meat, and potatoes.

From Akron to Mentor to Lakewood folks lined up for birthdays, anniversaries, graduations, engagements, hot first dates, or just a good steak and martini. Joining the folks were some dandies from near and far. Quoting Les Roberts introduction: "Industrialists and corporate CEOs, some were reporters, and cops, laborers, a few dedicated imbibers, and a regular group of men who always lunched there [JIM'S] with attractive women who weren't their wives . . ."

Reasons for JIM'S draw abound: Steaks were choice, drinks were stiff, service was tops, and Ray Rockey's sculling skills were close to the bone. Add to that the glue holding it all together was the Lady PhD from Hard Knocks U.–the former Mrs. Kerkles, Queen of the Flats, Mrs. Jim, A.K.A. Hilda T. Mercurio.

It comes as no surprise, Hilda and Frank's fortune rising like a twenty-loaf batch of yeasted dough, they sold the county home on Pleasant Valley Road, packed up and moved to

Frank and Hilda's Van Aken house

FROM THE BACK OF THE HOUSE

more plush digs in Shaker Heights.

The two-story red brick on Van Aken Boulevard was a happy house infused with Aunt Hilda's hospitality, Uncle Frank's class, and Aunt Mickey's charm . . .

Hold it! Who is Aunt Mickey?

Goes like this: Ethel May McCue (not technically an Aunt), employed at a downtown Cleveland bank, met regularly with Hilda concerning the business of JIM'S. Over the months, business mixing with chit chat, a bond established, Hilda revealed she had diabetes, daily injected herself with insulin. Some time thereafter, a regular bank meeting missed, Hilda hospitalized, released was in need of full time live-in domestic help. Came to mind Ethel McCue and an offer was made: Frank and Hilda would pay her a salary, she would live with them, travel, every thing.**

As it turned out, Mickey accepted the offer, became Aunt Mickey to the clan (Ray called her Dolly) and was there for everything including, when needed, hostessing JIM'S lunch and dinner hours.

Aunt Mickey hosting at JIM'S

FROM THE BACK OF THE HOUSE

Back to the Shaker Heights' House–a family gathering place, Aunt Hilda cooked, Aunt Mickey helped, and Uncle Frank (a 16-mm film buff) showed home movies in the basement. Children, grandchildren, relatives and friends gathered for birthdays, holidays, and off the cuff special events to snack, drink, dine, talk, and watch Frank's movies.

Skipping ahead again (that chronological thing) a few years hence, Ray dating his second wife to be (my mother Evelyn Rose, more later), I made my first trip to the "big city" and the Shaker Heights house. (I lived with Evelyn Rose's parents, Ida and Rosar Ferra in Creekside, Pennsylvania, population around 1000.) It was at the Shaker house that I was introduced to Aunt Hilda and company for a get acquainted meeting.

Thinking about it fifty years later, it might have been so Frank and Hilda could check out the nine-year old kid from P.A. to be sure he didn't have rickets, club feet, some green mold between his toes.

As it turned out, test passed, there were regular Christmas, Easter, long weekends, and summer vacation forays to the big city via bus or with Aunts and Uncles. On the visits, Ray living downtown above JIM's, Evelyn Rose (ah hum) rooming in an apartment off Scranton, yours truly stayed at the Shaker Heights house with Aunt Hilda, Uncle Frank, and Aunt Mickey.

FROM THE BACK OF THE HOUSE

Initially like childhood incursions into some rich neighbor's back yard (imagine Marco Polo when he first saw chop sticks), becoming assimilated into a new world of wealth, luxury and indoor plumbing, one soon learned, regardless of the event, whatever the occasion, talked about in and around prime rib, pasta, Frank's cinema art, and/or duck ala orange, was *the* Steak House.

From, How'd we do ($$$)last night, to the price of beef, to the sick, healthy, stealing or otherwise "help," to a rude customer's remark, to cutting the grass, to towels in the rest rooms–the clan's crown jewel was Jim's Steak House.

One also learned, though Raymond was entrusted with running the jewel, Aunt Hilda was President and CEO and Uncle Frank ate (peeled for him by Hilda, no kidding) seedless grapes.

---

*See end note #2 for more on Winsor French

**One of the every things (no joke) had Mickey, in the mornings, warming Uncle Frank's coffee cup by running hot water over it. The mug warmed, she filling it with hot joe. Frank liked things, coffee included, fresh and very hot.

Jim's STEAK HOUSE

14
THREE STRIKES

Eating seedless grapes peeled by Hilda, Frank's Standard Excavating office was not far from JIM'S 1800 Scranton Road address. Driving from Shaker Heights, he regularly dropped his grape peeler at *the* Steak House before beginning his appointed rounds around Cleveland. Later in the day, he and

Two Frank's Standard Excavating Company Headquarters

a few cronies would pop in JIM'S for a noon time snack where, depending on Raymond's priority for the day, Aunt Hilda might be hosting lunch, seating customers, handing out menus, and/or answering the phone. To the casual observer it might appear she was helping Raymond. In reality,

FROM THE BACK OF THE HOUSE

having done every job at JIM'S (including time at the meat saw) she knew who did what, where, and when, from the front, back, basement and upstairs of the house. Not only that, she counted every full plate that came out of the kitchen, every dirty spoon that went in, knew which restroom needed soap, where every penny was hidden and dollar folded. And why not, she owned the joint. Matter of fact, whether working, visiting, having dinner or just hanging out, Hilda pretty much, within a dollar, could give you the cha-ching take for the week even before she glanced at the daily balance sheet.

Along those lines, her eyes on everything from the till to restroom soap, she still managed to see gnat specks on the

Circa 1953, Hilda (third from left) and the JIM'S "girls"

JIM'S "girl's" white uniforms, white shoes too!* No three strikes and you're out with Hilda. One was it and it better not happen again.

On the strike-out dictum, an exception: "my boy" got the benefit of close calls, usually ending up with a three-ball walk. Understandable. Remember, he being the son she never had (despite Frank's grape peeling status), owned the ump.

One of Ray's close calls that didn't muster a walk (he struck out) was a family closet footnote and not much talked about. A shrug, missed it, don't know, had Raymond, somewhere around 1947, betrothed to a certain Dorothy A. Radke.

Mr. and Mrs. Raymond Rockey I

Strike three came not many months after the blessed event took place. Seems something (three guesses first two don't count) hit the fan, splattered, a divorce ensued and Mrs. Dot Rockey flew the coop. Raymond's home the apartment

FROM THE BACK OF THE HOUSE

above JIM'S, (all Ray's Misses flew the coop, think about it, he worked downstairs) he stayed put. Some speculate the reason for the divorce had something to do with the Navy myth about "one in every port." Others think it had something to do with a Raymond fixation on distaff panties. To wit: His stock remark to ladies of all stripes, "I'm going to get in your panties") seems he explored the drawers of one or two ladies in every port. Reasons for the pantie fascination will never be fully known but, in some murky Freudian soup, something dark dogged him. Either that or the wiring in his "species preservation makeup" ended up in fast forward mode.

Author Les Roberts', describing a fictional character in his novel, *The Irish Sports Pages* **, hints at the malady:
> The son of a bitch had to fuck her ... because there are some men like that–married or not–men who, because of whatever demons live within the deepest shadows of their souls, have to score with every woman who crosses their path. They don't have to love her, or like her, or even be particularly attracted to her. They just have to have her. For the challenge of it–the thrill of the hunt. For the heady rush of conquest. For the variety, for bragging rights, for another notch on their bedpost.
> For fun.
> And because in some way it validates them.

Whatever, Dot Radken history, the luck shysters plotting and/or the fate ladies spinning, the Cleveland Indians were

FROM THE BACK OF THE HOUSE

about to win the 1948 World Series. Add to the brew, a nineteen-year-old mother of one (me), Evelyn Rose (Ferra) Marsico, stepped off Creekside, Pennsylvania to Cleveland, Ohio Greyhound bus.

---

*Early on the uniforms were starched white, like nurses used to wear. Later in the 1980's the uniforms were black and white pants' suit affairs that favored Weight Watcher ladies. Alas, a few of the "girls" had missed a Watcher's meeting or two.

**THE IRISH SPORTS PAGES, Les Roberts, page 162, St. Martin's press 2002

PART II
HELP WANTED

15

WAITRESS WANTED, ALL SHIFTS

Skipping back, Evelyn Rose in a stormy marriage to Creekside's own Jim Marsico (the young couple were on/off separated and/or married three time from around 1942 to 1949), when she stepped off that Greyhound bus in Cleveland she had left (as previously mentioned) her seven-year old son (me) behind with her parents/my grandparents in Creekside, Pennsylvania.

Arrived in Cleveland, Evelyn Rose moved in with a girlfriend and landed a so-so waitress job at a Chinese restaurant. Soon after deciphering column one from column two, with the smell of moo goo gai pan up her nose, an ad in the Cleveland Press's HELP WANTED section caught her eye:

JIM'S STEAK HOUSE
waitress wanted, all shifts
phone CHERRY 8784

In some kind of Jim gobbledegook horoscope (get it JIM'S, Jim Marsico) she called the Cherry number and Ray answered:

"Jim's Steak House."

"Hello, I saw your ad for a waitress . . ."

"Any experience."

"Yes."

"Where?"

She told him the Chinese Restaurant.

"Any place else?"

FROM THE BACK OF THE HOUSE

"Ah, Capital Restaurant."

"Where's that?"

"Ah, Indiana Pennsylvania . . ."

"What's your phone number?"

She gave him the number.

Ray: "All filled up right now, don't call me, I'll call you."

The next morning, Evelyn riding to work on a city bus, sat next to a nice lady. A conversation struck up, nice lady happened to work at Jim's Steak House, a waitress, was going, even as they spoke, to her appointed rounds at the restaurant. They talked some more. Evelyn told her she had seen the JIM'S want ad for a waitress, had called, talked to some man. Nice lady said, "Musta been Aunt Hilda's golden 'my boy', Raymond, he runs the joint." The bus stopped at the corner of Scranton and Carter Road, nice lady got off.

Later that morning, story goes, nice lady sipping coffee before the noon lunch rush with the JIM'S "girls," Raymond came down from his upstairs perch and, as was his custom, joined the group. Chatting, the nice lady from the bus told Ray, "Funny thing happened on the way to work."

Ray: "What's that?"

"Sat next to some egg roll slinger, said she called here about a waitress job."

He talked to so many.

Bus lady said, "Name was Evelyn Rose, a real looker."

FROM THE BACK OF THE HOUSE

Tripping over cups and saucers, Ray made haste to his office. Going through many wrinkled scraps of paper in his waste basket, a scrawled phone number next to *Evelyn Rose* retrieved, he sat behind his desk and (back then you didn't press) dialed the number.

Evelyn Rose answered, "Hello."

"This is Ray Rockey, Jim's Steak House, you called about a job."

"Oh yes . . ." and it went from there.

In an interview Evelyn Rose recounts what transpired: "Next day I took a bus to JIM'S and somebody at the front sent me to the cocktail lounge. I waited and waited. Finally Ray came out, cock of the walk, tying his neck tie. After the usual chit chat, sniffing around, he asked me if I could tend bar. Never behind a bar in my life, didn't know Scotch from moon shine, I said sure and got the job."

The planets lined up in some kind of Pennsylvania, Cleveland, JIM triangle, Evelyn Rose went to work at Jim's Steak House same time the Cleveland Indians were playing the Boston Braves in the World Series, fall of 1948.

As it turns out, the Series a boon (Indians won the series four games to two), record setting 85,000 plus home game fans at Municipal Stadium, JIM'S not only packed them in, fans hung (back then you could drink, drive, walk, ride a bike, scratch in public, and most everybody did) from the

FROM THE BACK OF THE HOUSE

ceiling. Cash register cha-chinging, Evelyn Rose hustling tables, Raymonds' heart panged in more ways than one.

16

Browns and Morse Code

In the days following the Indian's 1948 World Series win, JIM'S cha-chinging at record levels, Evelyn Rose waiting on tables, the Browns' football season under way, "my boy" made his move:

Ray to Evelyn Rose: "You like football?"

Evelyn Rose not sure if they used a bat or a basket in football, "Oh yes, I like football."

Ray explains to small town Pennsylvania girl, "There's a local team, won a few championships, the Browns, some of the players brake bread here at JIM'S."

"How wonderful."

"Have two tickets, wondered if she would like to go to the game this Sunday."

Evelyn Rose, all fluttery, "Oh, yes, love to . . . but . . ."

"What?"

"I don't' think so."

"Why not?"

"Ah, I . . . I . . . I don't have anyone to go with me, couldn't use two tickets."

Ray rolls his eyes, "I MEANT for YOU to go with ME!"

Demurely: "Oh, in that case, sure."

Don't look now but "my boy" had just swallowed, not only the hook, but line, sinker, and rod too.

A few weeks after the Brown's date, Aunt Hilda and Uncle

FROM THE BACK OF THE HOUSE

Frank having dinner at *the* Steak House, Evelyn Rose (Ray made "girl" table assignments) waited on the Shaker Heights duo. In an aside moment, Aunt Hilda mentioned to Ray, "That a nice girl waiting on us, where'd you get her?"

Ray, swallowing a canary grin, beckoned Evelyn Rose table side. Smiles, chuckles, introductions, wham bam thank you mam. Evelyn passed the mustard and soon thereafter she possessed not only the Morse Code (security firm) password for Jim's Steak House but Frank and Hilda's Shaker Heights' home as well.

17

NUPTIAL BLISS, ALMOST

Courtship in full bloom, Ray living in the three bedroom apartment above JIM'S, the official record has Evelyn Rose residing in an apartment, in her words, "Up off Scranton, not that far. Ray gave me lifts to and from work."

No blushing please.

Evelyn Rose, waited tables, recalled those early day at JIM's: "The back room help consisted of one cook and a dishwasher. No bartender at the lunch hour, the 'girls' filled customers' drink orders themselves. We also bussed (removed dirty dishes/utensils and reset with clean) our own tables . . . at dinner hour, a bartender on duty, Ray seated customers with an eye to spreading tips for us 'girls'. On busy nights a waitress could make three-hundred bucks a night in tips."

Which incidentally, justified the "girls" nine dollars a week (1950's upped to around $40.00 a week in the 90's) salary.

Evelyn Rose further related, "If an employee didn't show up for whatever, me or Ray filled the gap. Some days, if two didn't show up we filled two gaps . . . got the job done."

Ray and Evelyn Rose dating for some eighteen months, in there somewhere Evelyn coup de graced (legally) hubby number one (Jim Marsico) and soon thereafter she and Ray set a September 1951 wedding date.

But set dates and weddings being what they are, a hitch: two weeks prior to the scheduled September ceremony Aunt

FROM THE BACK OF THE HOUSE

Hilda came down with pneumonia. Some speculate stress was the culprit. Remember "my boy's" first marriage was a flash-in-the-pan disaster. Maybe stress is not the right word. How's panic?

Whatever, penicillin and rationalization working (Hilda always seemed to come up with an excuse for Raymond's peccadillos, Peck's bad boy meant well) the wedding was reset for December 29.

This time on schedule, the ceremony (conducted by a Justice of the Peace) took place in the living room of Ray's apartment above JIM'S. Aunt Hilda, Uncle Frank, Aunt Micky, a hand full of relatives from Pennsylvania, and a few of Hilda and Frank's Cleveland cronies witnessed the event. Standing as best man–Ray's Benedictine High School buddy (he now worked full time at JIM'S), Tony Liotta. Evelyn Rose's sister from PA, Mary Morganti, was the bridesmaid.

Evelyn Rose

Evelyn Rose's Pennsylvania hometown newspaper (Indiana Evening Gazette, Indiana PA, circa December 1951) ran the story on its society page:

Ferra-Rocky (the paper spells Rockey wrong, a hint of things to come) Nuptials in Cleveland

FROM THE BACK OF THE HOUSE

On Saturday, December 29, at half after three in the afternoon in Cleveland, Ohio, the wedding of Evelyn Ferra, daughter of Mr. and Mrs. Rosar Ferra of Creekside, Pa and Raymond Rockey, son [kinda] of Mr. and Mrs. Frank Mercurio of 3057 Van Aken Boulevard, Shaker Heights, Cleveland, Ohio took place in the beautiful new home ["my boy's apartment above JIM'S] of the bride and groom . . . following the ceremony a reception for 100 guests was held at Jim's Steak House in Cleveland. Mr. Rocky [that spelling hint again] is manager of the Steak House . . . Among the out of town guests were . . . Gary Lee Ferra [me, changed from Marsico] . . . of Creekside.

To prove this isn't fiction, an after-wedding photo is here displayed.

Further proof is one of several photos taken of a reception dinner (family and friends only)

L-R Mary, Evelyn, Ray, Tony

FROM THE BACK OF THE HOUSE

which took place downstairs in the Steak House's PD (private dining) room.

Top L-R: Hilda, back of Frank Jr's head, Evelyn, Ray, bridesmaid Mary (kid with cracker guess who)

JIM'S main dining room, lounge, and bar remained open for business.

Alas, who could have known, in all the warmness of the occasion, not one elf dancing on a champaign bottle's cork could have guessed, approximately ten years later, in the stench of alcohol-induced debauch, the nuptial bliss would end like an empty bottle of cheap gin. But that's skipping ahead, the "almost" came first.

18
RAY'S APARTMENT

The wedding over, no time for a honeymoon, Evelyn Rose (now Mrs. Rockey number 2 and no longer incognito) had officially moved to Ray's apartment above JIM'S. The happy couple, after "working day and night" at JIM'S, partied in hot spots all over Cleveland.

Evelyn Rose (lower right) enjoying the "Ray" show at a Cleveland club

A word or two about the 1950's version of Ray's cozy apartment: you got up to the swanky flat by way of a heavy brown door (sometimes locked sometimes open) located in the short hallway between the JIM'S kitchen and cocktail bar. The door led to a narrow stairwell with twenty or so steps covered with cocoa colored carpet. Navigating the steps you

FROM THE BACK OF THE HOUSE

made your way around (stored there by Ray) broken dishes, cups, neckties, sales slips, shoes, cuff links and assorted stuff that might have some amateur shrink speculating that the clutter signaled something dark, deep, and menacing.

Whatever, up and around all the clutter, at the top of the stairs the same cocoa wall-to-wall carpet continued into a short hallway.

To the left was Ray's office complete with mahogany desk, casting sofa, and sky light. At the end of the hall was a full bath between a master and a smaller bedroom. The master bedroom (where Ray and Mrs. slept) had a door to an outside cement staircase and featured, through double picture windows, a nice view of the Cuyahoga, Higbees (1950's), and the Terminal Tower. The smaller bedroom offered a view of JIM'S tarred roof, next door neighbor Mohawk Trucking, and Carter Road.

Across the hallway from Ray's office, a living/dining/kitchen* area (imagine a modest hotel suite) offered up yet another view of the Cuyahoga and Cleveland's Skyline. Before Uncle Frank shook everything up in later years, this was the only air-conditioned spot in the building.

A few steps from the living room, a second full bath serviced a third bedroom which overlooked the Cleveland Fire Department's Station #21 and Eagle Ramp Bridge.

Furnishings throughout the apartment (sofas, chairs,

FROM THE BACK OF THE HOUSE

Living/Dining area with 4X5 kitchen to the right behind TV and glass block

beds, drapes) resembled the TV set of the 1950's *I Love Lucy* show.

Sullying the TV motif a bit, Morse Code silver tape glistened on all windows. The tape could best be described as duck tape cut into 1/4 inch strips and glued to the window in some kind of abstract painting rectangular design.

The reason for the security: address 1800 Scranton Road, The Flats, bottom of Eagle Ramp–JIM'S had a load of overnight cash laying around not to mention rum, rye, gin, wine, beer and a ton of choice beef.

Funny thing, except for one time, JIM'S never got robbed.

FROM THE BACK OF THE HOUSE

The story goes: Ray and Evelyn Rose were out somewhere for a Sunday (JIM'S closed Sundays) dinner. Gone for a few hours, they returned to discover a broken window in Ray's office. The office trashed, money stolen, the police summoned, no one was ever caught. Ray always suspected (the help knew where Saturday night cash was stashed) an inside job. In any case, day after the break in Ray hired a brick layer and the window's view of the JIM'S roof became a 4x5 rectangular red brick crook-proof patch in the wall.

---

*In years to come Ray would install a sliding glass door that opened from his apartment dining area to the roof over JIM'S main dining room. The roof served up spectacular views of the Cuyahoga, Terminal Tower, Tower City and Jacobs Fields. Most important, in spring, summer, and fall, it offered Raymond a private place to party, drink, eat, drink, party, drink, entertain, watch the Cuyahoga boat traffic and drink.

19

A ROLL AND HOT CAKES

In the 50's, Rock and Roll making its debut in the music world, Cleveland was on a roll of its own: in sports the Cleveland Indians fielded Feller, Lemon, Wynn, Colavito, and rookie of the year Herb Score. * Not to be outdone, Paul Browns' football teams ruled the NFL with greats like Otto Graham, Lou Groza, and Danti Lavelli. In politics, Mayor Thomas A. Burke (Burke Lakefront Airport) was about to be succeeded by the rising Stella MIA, Anthony Colubris.

Enjoying the uptown glow, JIM'S phone number changed to Cherry (CH) 1-4454, Ray added more "girls" to wait on tables, hired a lunchtime bartender, and presented a new

---

A LA CARTE
· MENU ·

The Steak you are to enjoy has been carefully selected, aged and prepared to fully satisfy your individual taste.

SHRIMP COCKTAIL . . . . 75¢

STEAKS

Large	3.50
Medium	3.00
Ground Top Sirloin	2.00
With Mushrooms . . . .75 extra per order	
With Onions . . . .50 extra per order	

Lamb Chops	2.50
Chicken (Broiled)	2.50
Fish (on Fridays)	1.50

Salad, Bread, Butter and Beverages included in All Dinners

ICE CREAM . . . . 20¢

CHEESE

Roquefort, with crackers	.35
Roquefort, dressing	.25

FROM THE BACK OF THE HOUSE

menu. The main attraction (what else) a Large Steak Dinner for $3.50, Medium, $3.00. Note Small Steak crossed out and stamped in is Shrimp Cocktail 75¢. More on that later.

Putting everything in proper perspective, a shot of Johnny Walker Black went for .75 cents. Take a look:

WINES AND LIQUORS

1.00	Apricot Delight	.75	Dubonnet	.60	Rob
.75	Alexander	.75	Bronx	.60	Old
.60	Bacardi	.65	Hunters	.75	Oran
.60	Brandy Cocktail	.65	Jack Rose	.65	Scarl
.60	Clover Club	.75	Manhattan	.60	Side
.75	Champagne Cocktail	1.00	Martini	.60	Sting
	Daiquiri Cocktail		.65		

S
.60	Sloe Gin Fizz	.65	Sherry Flip	.65	Cubc
.60	Silver Fizz	.75	Whiskey Sour	.60	Plant
.60	Golden Fizz	.75	Brandy Sour	.75	Ange
.60	Royal Fizz	.75	John Collins	.60	Crem
.60	New Orleans Fizz	.75	Singapore Gin Sling	.75	(G1
	Porto Rican Rickey	.60	Gin Daisy	.60	

ALS — IMPORTED CORDIALS

	Pony			Pony	
Curacao	.50	Creme de Cacao		.60	B & B
Kuemmel	.50	Creme de Menthe, green or white		.60	V. C. Vieille C
Triple Sec	.60	Cointreau		.75	Benedictine
Anisette	.60	Drambuie		.75	Kahlua (Licor
Drink	.60	Rock & Rye	Drink	.50	C & B
		Grand Marnier		85	

H AND IRISH WHISKEY

	.65	Johnny Walker, Red Label	.65	King's Ransom
	.65	Johnny Walker, Black Label	.75	Ballantine's
	.65	Haig & Haig, 5 Star	.65	Cutty Sark
	.65	Haig & Haig, Pinch Bottle	.75	Dewar's White
White Horse		.65	John Jameson & Son (Irish Whiskey)	

Ray in beef and .75 cents a shot heaven, Evelyn Rose

FROM THE BACK OF THE HOUSE

filling gaps, not to be outdone, Aunt Hilda got a little drum roll of her own. An article in the Cleveland Press, Ship & Shore, May 5, 1952 by Julian Griffin:

She's Just "Mrs. Jim" to Her Water-Front Pals

A picture of waterfront personalities is incomplete unless you include "Mrs. Jim." as she is called by her waitresses and patrons at Jim's Steak House on the west bank of the Cuyahoga River at Collision Bend.

"Mrs. Jim," whose real name is Hilda, started the place in 1929, on a small scale, serving maybe five steaks a day. In those days she did practically all the work, from cutting the meat and cooking to scrubbing floors "in the wee small hours."

Today she is on the job every day, but things are much easier for her as the prosperous and efficient organization serves 300 to 400 people daily . . .

"Mrs. Jim," who stands 5 ft., 11 in. and is plenty able to take care of herself at all times, serves only steaks and chops, with fish on Friday—no soups, vegetables or fancy desserts. And people from all over beat a path to her door.

"A few weeks ago a couple of Englishmen came in," she related. "They said the last thing before leaving London someone told them to be sure to

FROM THE BACK OF THE HOUSE

> eat a meal at Jim's Steak House. And when they were ready to return home, by air, they had me pack a couple of steaks in dry ice. Said they wanted to show the folks back home the size of steaks served in this country."
> Manager of the place is Raymond Rockey, whom she calls "my boy." Son of her dead sister, she reared him since he was four years old.
> For a good many years men only dined there. About three years ago ladies started coming also. Now they are installing a powder room.

Speaking of powder rooms, some speculate the ladies' pit stop was under "my boys" personal care and supervision. Others swear by it.

Regarding the limited menu items in Griffin's article, Aunt Hilda was skeptical about messing up what had got her to here. I.e., JIM'S was a meat and potato place. When anybody asked for fish (other than special days), Hilda's reply, "This is a steak house, you want fish go to a fish house."

Years later, Ms. Escargot of the Plain Dealer (November 25, 1966) put it this way, "The menu is straight from the shoulder, merely stating the name of the dish and its price. No mention made of the chef's pedigree and how many spring of parsley went into the garnish . . ."

And yet another reviewer's (Gus Utter**) take:

> Mrs. Jim and her manager, Raymond Rockey . . . serve only such manly provender as steak, ham, lamb chops and the like, and trout or

FROM THE BACK OF THE HOUSE

other fish on special days. Customers may have any kind of potatoes they want so long as they are the hash brown variety because that's all the establishment serves. There is no soup, no salad excepting head lettuce with dressing, and no pastry. The only other vegetables allowed on the premise are onions, which are french fried in rings, and mushrooms if they are classified as vegetables.

Regarding Hilda's clamp on limited menu items, she and Frank on one of their many Sarasota Florida vacations (they had friends there, would later build a house there), one night Ray and Evelyn Rose decided to try something new on the menu–shrimp cocktail. Why not. As Evelyn Rose put it, "First thing next morning Ray drove over to State Fish, bought a few pounds of shrimp, brought them back, cooked them up, put 'em on ice. I made a shrimp sauce, extra horseradish added for Ray, he liked things spicy, and that afternoon Ray rubber-stamp (noted above)on all the JIM'S menus."

That evening, dinner guests arriving, Ray announced, as he seated them, the all-new to JIM'S menu, a seafood appetizer.

Reported by Evelyn Rose, the first offering of shrimp to have gone "Like hot cakes," the next day Ray bought an extra pound of shrimp. Evelyn Rose: "Same thing, went like hot cakes."

Sure enough, a month later, Hilda back from the

FROM THE BACK OF THE HOUSE

Sunshine State, after being shown the profit made on shrimp, insisted the tasty crustacean became a JIM'S permanent addition. About the menu additions, Evelyn Rose said, "Same thing happened with fried onion rings. Hilda out of town, rings added to the menu, went like hot cakes."

So much for hot cakes.

A thief in the night lurked just around the corner.

---

*Herb Score debuted with the Indians in 1955. He won 16 games in his first season. In 1956 he won 20. Compared to Whitey Ford, Sandy Kofax, May 7, 1957 in a game with the Yankees, Gil McDougal hit a line drive, and Whittier's, "What Might Have Been," had new meaning. 2006 Herb was inducted into the Cleveland Indian's Hall of Fame. After a long illness, Herb passed in November 2008.

**The Gus Utter article in the JIM'S scrap book, if the publisher's name is known to anyone please send info to me, Wikipedia or both.

20

A Thief in the Night

Amid all the menu changes at JIM'S, the summer of '52 blending into autumn, Cleveland Press reviewer, critic, and bon vivant man about town, Winsor French, pulled his Rolls Royce into JIM'S parking lot and popped in for dinner.

Greeted by Ray (Winsor's reputation preceded him), seated at a choice table, the presence of epicure reviewer French in the house whispered to the JIM'S staff, Ray lavished hospitality reserved for a god on the gastronome critic.

A few days later, Thursday, August 21, 1952 a review by Winsor in The Cleveland Press hit the streets:

> Jim's Steak House on Collision Bend in the Flats, which I at last found my way to, could easily become one of the most exciting and spectacular restaurants in the country. If, that is, someone would only use a little inexpensive imagination.
> The view across its sweeping lawn of the twisting river, massive bridges soaring overhead and the Terminal Tower leaping up from the jagged skyline in the farther distance, is absolutely breathtaking.

FROM THE BACK OF THE HOUSE

Yes, instead of making any attempt at bringing the panorama into the rooms, a very conscious effort seems to have been made to shut it out. The windows are too high to look out of comfortably from the tables; furthermore they have been screened by awnings.
Opaque glass brick prevents the elbow benders from watching the dramatic river traffic from the bar and within another year or so the prospering weeping willows on the lawn will have succeeded in closing out the view entirely. How anyone could turn their back on such fantasy is beyond the limits of my understanding. A reasonably small sum of money could transform the restaurant in nothing flat to something every bit as startling as the famous Rivera high above the Hudson in Manhattan, or even the Top of the Mark in San Francisco.
Drive down there some evening and see for yourself. You will come away wondering why they don't at least scatter a few tables about on the terrace.
Well, there it is, the steaks at least, are excellent, the drinks are just as good and the prices won't cripple you. And if you will stretch your neck a little you will be able to see the draw bridges slowly lifting against the sky to let the freighters pass down the river. The beauty and the magic are there all right, some only has to reach out and grab it.

Winsor's lampoon a thief in the night, the JIM'S brain trust (Hilda, Frank, and Ray) sat grim and tight lipped around

FROM THE BACK OF THE HOUSE

the Shaker Height's house kitchen table. The French article read, reread, chewed over, and read again, the brain trust swallowing hard the gloomy contents. After some time, grim giving way to tight lips, she could hold it no longer, Aunt Hilda broke wind, "Reach out and grab my ass . . . hayseed critic with a wild hair up his nose." Frank, strong silent type (no doubt having Sicilian woodshed thoughts) said little while Ray lamented the hospitality he had lavished on the (unprintable) bon vivant dinner guest.

A dozen Rob Roys later, Winsor's critique stuffed in a garbage can, life went on. But in the JIM'S air, like the smell of rendering animal fat, the criticism simmered along with bruised egos in waiting.

21

IN THE MEANTIME, JIM'S DAILY ROUTINE

The Winsor French "reach and grab it" article bumping around in *the* Steak House brain trust's bruised egos, JIM'S daily routine went on as usual.

The routine started, fifty-two weeks a year, Monday through Saturday, 5:30 a.m. sharp, when Tony Liotta unlocking the back door to let in the kitchen crew.

You remember Tony. He and Ray graduated Benedictine High together, Ray's best man at wedding two to Evelyn Rose. Elevated to Assistant Manager of JIM'S, Tony became one of the clan, broke bread, shared meals, dated one of Ray's ex wives, got fired . . . but that's for later.

His personal life a tangle, a marriage ended in some kind of Catholic annulment, he became an altar boy at around forty plus, serving midnight Mass at St. Michael's Catholic Church on Scranton Road.

Regarding shared meals: Tony a devout Catholic, inevitably it came to pass (no-fish a one-time Catholic Friday tradition) that one Friday morning he moseyed upstairs to the JIM'S apartment where Evelyn Rose was making bacon and eggs for yours truly. Want some? Sure. He sat and began to eat. Mouth full of bacon, second or third bite, gagging, he shot to his feet, spit half-chewed bacon onto his plate. It was Friday!

Evelyn Rose some mix of once removed Protestant (as was

FROM THE BACK OF THE HOUSE

I) slightly amused, said, "How was I to know?"

Tony stormed off downstairs, it was her fault. They bonded thereafter and later became serious friends. More on that later but suffice it to say, Tony would become a tragic player in JIM'S Act III.

Tony, crew cut black hair (when he just shaved it didn't look like he shaved), could have been a guard on any college football team in the country. Tony's office (about the size of a Volkswagen Van) was next to JIM'S kitchen entrance from which he honchoed the back of the

Tony

house, ordered supplies, and took inventory. His front of the house duties included hosting JIM'S lunch (dinner if Ray wanted a night off) and filling in for sick or tardy bartenders.

Continuing the JIM'S morning routine: first things had the scullers mopping, cleaning, sweeping; cooks chopping potatoes, cutting meat; and Tony prepping a stainless steel urn for the brewing of around three gallons of Haserot Companies' finest bean coffee.

Around 7:30 a.m., things humming along, Ray pattered downstairs in slippers, T-shirt, and jeans. Cigarette between lips, he drew a cup of still brewing coffee, checked in with Tony about day to day–who was doing who, where, and

FROM THE BACK OF THE HOUSE

when–then made his way back upstairs to his office where he began a count of last night's take.

Around 10:00 a.m. the "girls" wandered in, went downstairs to their basement room lockers, and changed into their JIM'S uniforms. Returned upstairs and before setting the tables for lunch (flat ware, paper napkins, no table clothes at lunch) they filled salt and pepper shakers. That done they gathered at a center table in the dinning room for coffee and a smoke. * Lighting up and between puffs there then took place an informal meeting–gripes, bitches, what went wrong yesterday, the good and the bad. Nothing was ever ugly at JIM'S. Okay, almost nothing.

Moving along, around 10:30 a.m., a notch up in the employees' food chain, the bartender arrived, lit up, and joined the "girls." Twenty or so minutes later the morning coffee confab ended and everybody readied for the lunch crowd which began dribbling in around 11:00 a.m..

Tony hosting lunch, Ray usually took off on errands. One of his favorite jaunts, the West Side Market, he shopped for produce, specialty items, and assorted fruits for Aunt Hilda.

Tagging along many times, entering the maze of market shops it was like some celebrity graced the aisles with vendors shouting: "Hey Ray! . . .Raymond, how ya doin! . . . Mr. Rockey! . . . Yooh, Mr. JIM'S," and Ray would buy a dozen this and dozen that and "Gimmy a sack of those."

FROM THE BACK OF THE HOUSE

A more favorite tag along trip with Ray was when he went buying beef for JIM'S. Ray knew all the meat packers around town and they knew him. Casually dressed, sauntering into a meat place, celebrity Ray, after some bantering with the head meat manager, was presented a handful of little red plastic JIM'S STEAK HOUSE sticks. The sticks were similar to those thing bartenders pierce martini olives with. JIM'S sticks in hand, a meat cooler door opened for him, Ray entered the just-above-freezing cooler where, from big hooks, hung row upon row of beef carcasses.

Making his way along the rows of beef, he selected loins he deemed fit for JIM'S. Loins in restauranteeze is the meat about three quarters of the way back, along and down from the vertebrae of a beef animal. Meat cutters fashion T-bone, strip, porterhouse, and tenderloin steaks from these loins.

Sticks in hand, Ray would walk along the rows of loins pressing each with a finger, shoving a stick into the beef that passed his mustard. The selected loins would then be trucked to Jim's Steak House where they were placed in JIM'S walk-in meat cooler. Daily when needed, a loin would be hauled out by JIM's cooks to face the kitchen steak saw.

Plain Dealer reviewer Fourchette Escargot put it this way: "The [JIM'S meat] cooler has been known to produce five-pound, two-inch thick blockbusters for a party of nine with no advance warning."

FROM THE BACK OF THE HOUSE

Continued Ms. Escargot: "[JIM'S] steaks are aged in a two-ton walk in cooler. After a period of confinement of from six to eight weeks in temp hovering around 32 degrees, they emerge tender and richly flavored." (Plain Dealer 11/25/66)

"Tender and richly flavored" is a nice way to put it. Basically it's beef left to ripen a bit before eating. It's a custom not confined to just man. More than a few wild animals prefer aged meat. All goes to taste, way back before fire, in the cave and so on, some like it more aged than others. Guess we're all from the same pot.

Ray back from his shopping jaunts, JIM'S lunch business winding down, he more than not ended up at the bar shmoozing with "liquid" lunch pals. There were dozens of such pals. One notable, Bob Hulderman, topped the list.

Bob far right at JIM'S bar. E. Rose/ Ray far left, an evening photo you get the idea

FROM THE BACK OF THE HOUSE

Bob, a salesman's salesmen, owned Cleveland's Commerce Ford Dealership for many years**. Bob and Ray had three things in common–booze, a Put-in Bay South Bass Island cottage, and booze.

The hop, skip, and a jump getaway (a prefab log cottage situated on a Lake Erie waterfront lot) provided a more private place to booze, hunt rabbits, duck, pheasant, party with "wild game" and generally (with wineries up to here) booze it up. And with Canada's Pelee Island (cheap whiskey by the case, Bob owned a twenty foot outboard Lyman) a one tank boat trip to the north, it was paradise found for the happy duo.

Water logged Polaroid of Ray and Bob in front of cottage

FROM THE BACK OF THE HOUSE

Another "liquid" pal of Ray's existed in bosom buddy Byron Laing. Byron was the sales manager for once locally famous P.O.C. (Pride of Cleveland) beer. A chain smoker shaped like an oak cask, his wide smile greeted anyone and everybody.

For the years Byron was at P.O.C , some swear Ray accounted for roughly 15 percent of the beer's bottom line.

Byron and Ray hung out together, went deer hunting in

Byron far left (guy in glasses?) Byron's wife Frankie, Evelyn Rose and Ray

Pennsylvania together, cavorted on Put-in-Bay together. And always, rain, shine, or snow, several cases of P.O.C. in tow, they skewered life.

For what it's worth, P.O.C. folded in 1954, Ray shopped

FROM THE BACK OF THE HOUSE

around and, after Byron's untimely death in 1960 (he was only 46), eventually switched to Amstel Light. Actually he drank almost anything with alcohol in it. In later years he would show up at family parties with several cases of Rolling Rock pony bottles, "Just to get started."

Anyway, the JIM'S lunch bunch melted away into a mellow afternoon, the daily JIM'S routine had the "girls" pulling up at a dinning room table. There they lit up, drank coffee and, amid chit chat of the day, counted tips. Tony left around 3:00 p.m. and the second shift came in around 4:00 p.m. to get ready for the dinner hour.

As to Ray, his "liquid" lunch over, he headed upstairs for what he called "a cat nap." The naps were anywhere from ten minutes to an hour depending on time available. In that regard, he was one of those guys who didn't need much sack time, was proud of it. "Going to sleep your life away" was his jab at any chump who got more than six hours sack time night or day.

---

* In the fifties everybody, almost, smoked. Later when no-smoking came into vogue (JIM'S closed before the 2007 Ohio Nazi-like total ban), JIM'S Carter Room was designatuniformed no smoking. The main dining room and lounge were light-up zones. No smoking or not, the "girls" would sneak to the back door to take a quick drag. Ray on the other hand, up until the end, kept a smoke fired up in an ashtray somewhere (usually at the bar) which he visited between hosting, chatting, and answering the house phone.

**From the original St Clair Ave location, Bob moved the dealership to Northfield Road in North Randall across the street from Randall Mall. Bob retired and the dealership closed in the early 80s.

22

CURTAIN UP, JIM'S DINNER HOUR, THE ROUTINE CONTINUED

Cat napped out, around 5:00 p.m., Ray began preening for his evening performance in his long running hit, "Hosting Dinner at JIM'S." Shower, shave, a freshly laundered shirt from Ames dry cleaners, tailored suit or sports jacket (in the fifties JIM'S required of males a coat and tie at the dinner hour), snappy Windsor knotted tie, shoes spit-shined, downstairs he'd go.

Entering the dinning room from the kitchen, as if on some unseen stage manager's cue, he took his position at a wood credenza close to the front entrance. A reservation book at finger tips, house phone at arms' reach, the show began with Ray hosting (remember his favorite movie was Casablanca, Café owner Rick, his idol) like a regular Humphry Bogart.

The Steak House Ray's stage, his nonstop evening shtick had him greeting and seating guests, handing out menus, reciting the specials of the day, closing with his patented, "And the steaks better be good."

Throughout the evening he visited diners, chatting, joking, schmoozing, sniffing the wind. Between sniffs, entrances and exits, there was always the house phone–Ray answering, talking, listening, jotting down, giving directions.

In between the above, he supervised everything from the heating/cooling thermostat (nobody better touch it), background music volume, to the dimming of the house

FROM THE BACK OF THE HOUSE

lights. In it all, he had a Lucky Strike going, parking the smoke in an ashtray between puffs.

Once in a while, responding to a phone call from some person looking for someone, he'd go to the kitchen, flip on the public address system and his voice crackled from the overhead dinning room speakers, "Phone call for J. Doe."

When he came back to the dinning room, J. Doe or no, like some blossoming radio announcer pleased with a first audition, he smiled, the waitresses smiled, the guests smiled. You could tell he liked it.

Occasionally, over the front-of-the-house's faint "elevator music," a loud crash would echo from the back of the house. Translation: somebody dropped a dish, cup, glass (or plural all of the above) in the kitchen.

Like a fire alarm had gone off, Ray bee-lined to catch the dropper. The perp apprehended, he recorded (usually on a skimp of paper or the inside of a book of JIM'S safety matches) a note outing the name of the offender, item or items broken, and the cost to be billed to the dropper.

The breakage scenario came from a Ray rule similar to an antique shop owner's warning, "If you break it, you own it." With Ray, you didn't own it, you (deducted from tips and/or pay check) paid for it.

Confirming his "pay for it" dictate, he'd smile and say, "You'd be surprised how it cuts down on breakage."

Alas, confirming what some said about Ray, "He had a

FROM THE BACK OF THE HOUSE

good heart," he'd pay back the dropper in a tip envelope a week or so later.

On another "lost-items" front, Ray never did figure out how to charge for stolen flatware (spoons, forks, knives) but he talked about some kind of metal detector at the front door. The idea got nixed when told how dippy that would look to arriving guests.

After the dinner rush slowed, around 9:00 p.m., Ray, Evelyn Rose, and yours truly usually ended up at a four-top close to Ray's host stand for dinner. As if on cue, a smiling waitress would show up and we'd order (guess what). Dinner served, Ray would continue his up and down, seating late dinner arrivals, tending to lingering guests, shooting the breeze with whoever came along.

Truth of the matter, Ray never sat, had a drink, ate dinner without getting up fifteen, twenty times or more. He consumed food between bites. Come to think of it, he lived life like that. But no regrets, he loved every minute, would have had it no other way.

Some evening, Aunt Hilda and Uncle Frank coming to *the* Steak House for dinner, the word went out to the JIM'S staff that the "Shaker Height duo" was on the way.

Double snap-to hanging in the air, reserved table, guess what they ate. Except one thing: Uncle Frank had to have his special order–onion diced into JIM'S hash brown potatoes.

FROM THE BACK OF THE HOUSE

The potato dish was not on the JIM'S menu but for Frank, well . . . hand on the tiller, remember.

On good nights (good nights for Ray were when people stood in line half way to Carter Road) customers leaving, Ray would smile with an engaging, "Thank yous (he said yous) good peoples." On slow nights (especially later on in the story) there was extra emphasis on, "Thank yous good peoples," with an added "Come back soon."

Good or bad night, things winding down, a late evening ritual had Ray going to the kitchen, nodding to the head cook. The nod known, gas stoves were turned off, uncooked meat and potatoes returned to walk in coolers, and the scullers began mopping (Ray insisted the kitchen be licking clean for the next day like the next day was for forever and no end in sight) the fat-slicked kitchen floor.

The final guests gone, the front door locked, it was necktie off for Ray and he'd hit the cocktail lounge for an un-winder or two with the bartender. Perched on his favorite stool at the end of the bar, a few of the "girls" usually joined in and, in the words of eyewitness Evelyn Rose, "Ray always said he waited for a little bell to go off, then he knew he had enough."

Ray's "waiting for a bell to go off" could last until who knows, knew, or remembered and the walls only knew who might get lucky on any given night.

23
FROM F TO R, ADOPTION, AND CHERRIES

Into the Ray/Evelyn Rose union a couple years, came October 15, 1954 and matters of adoption took center stage. Namely, yours truly (just turned thirteen), on one of those forays from Pennsylvania to Ohio, was escorted by Ray and Evelyn Rose to the court room of Cleveland probate judge Walter Kinder. After answering a few questions from the Judge, next thing I knew there were three Rockeys in the JIM'S family–Ray, Evelyn Rose, and guess who.

The immediate more memorable results were two: alphabetical seating being what it is in grade school–F(Ferra) to R(Rockey)–twenty seats back wasn't all that bad. And, instead of staying at the Shaker Heights' house when in Cleveland, the apartment above the Steak House became home away from home. Here began an introduction to the front and back of the house, and is probably in part the reason you're reading this book.

Not sure what it meant (whose sure what any of it means), families (Ferra, Mercurio) of both sides (far as you could tell by outward appearance/comments between the lines) seemed to think the whole package (marriage/adoption) was a good thing and turns out it was . . . for a while . . . but that's for later.

A little off track, but one wonders how it all fits in, what you would have been, is there a plan, or is this all random chance? In a larger sense, speaking of random and fitting in,

FROM THE BACK OF THE HOUSE

some look at the images sent back to earth by the Mars landers and marvel at the wonder of it all. Others think how barren, bleak, lifeless for millions of years Mars just sat there, sits there now, collecting dust while earthlings moved mountains around, came up with cell phones, the internet, and the Hubble telescope.

Which further leads others to wonders: if anybody, half baked advanced as we are, is out there they must be looking out there too and you'd think (both lookers looking) somebody would connect the dots. Then again, given the present global general state of well being, maybe somebody found us, took a look, and put us on their "no-call" list.

Wondering aside, shortly after becoming an adopted Rockey, while helping Ray take JIM'S inventory (Ray called items out, I wrote it down) yours truly spelled "cherries" something like "chairyes." The botched spelling proved to be a life changer when the "chairyes" spelling was shown around to Hilda and Frank. Things going downhill from there, August 1955, Gilmour Academy, Gates Mills, Ohio saw it's first non-Catholic student, me. It's another long story but short of it, meeting with the Headmaster, keeping my shaky Gilmour student statue patched up, Ray spent more time at Gilmour than some of the Brothers of Holy Cross faculty. As it turned out, Ray's ambassador efforts (including bottles of expensive Scotch) didn't work. After two years I packed it in and returned to Pennsylvania to complete high school. The whole

FROM THE BACK OF THE HOUSE

thing is a comedic farce reserved for funeral parlor chats.

In the meantime, time flew and around 1956 the only Flats' neighbors around JIM'S being Mohawk Trucking Company, Cleveland Fire Station #21, Eagle Ramp Bridge, and a zillion sea gulls, Uncle Frank and Aunt Hilda decided to shake it up a little.

24
Shake Up

The '50s a time (before the media got wind of cholesterol) when steak was nice and before, after, or in between three martinis separated the men (a few ladies too) from the boys, Cleveland touted itself, "the best location in the nation." Population a million plus, beaucoup jobs, money burning holes in whatever, dining-out ended up on many people's list of things to do.

No surprise, JIM'S choice cuts of beef, golden hash browns, onion rings, stout drinks, and impeccable service topped many people's registry of places to eat, imbibe, entertain.

Alas, with the boon, JIM'S cha-chings deafening, truckloads of cash daily passing through "my boy's" hands, Aunt Hilda's other boy, Uncle Frank (he had "eyes" everywhere, especially on the "golden goose" that was JIM'S) hatched a plan. Taking Hilda aside, in twenty-four karat capisce, he laid it all out (all is relative, he loved "my boy" too but he had gotten word of the late night parties at JIM'S) that a better way behind door number three lay.

Franks' capisce irrefutable, Hilda agreed and a short time thereafter Frank took "my boy" for a ride. The offer Ray couldn't refuse was simple: new neighbors he would a-soon be having. In even plainer capisce, Frank and Hilda were selling their Shaker Heights' house and building an addition (more of a penthouse) on top of the umteen unused square

FROM THE BACK OF THE HOUSE

feet above *the* Steak House, "right next door" to "my boy's" apartment.

It doesn't take a Harry Stack Sullivan to imagine what flashed through "my boy's" mind as he calculated the new home-address for Frank, Hilda, and Aunt Mickey.

Let's just say he blotched up red and smiled as many little boogie man strutted through his hash brown potatoes.

Think about it. All those years (albeit sharing with James Kerkles) "my boy" had basked in Aunt Hilda's adopted son-ship shining armor. When James died, he not only basked in her glow, he baked in it. Then along comes this goombah from Murray Hill and Raymond had to share Hilda all over again. He could live with that, but holy smokes! Now Tootsie and Frank (up until now miles away in Shaker Height's boondocks, they couldn't hear a peep let alone Ray and his cronies howling at the moon) would be camped next door, know when "my boy" sneezed, clipped his toe nails and, along with the flies on the wall, follow the JIM'S cash flow.

Things kaput, Ray stuck in whatayagonnado dilemmasville, making maters down-the-drain worse, Aunt Hilda owned the kit and caboodle purse, and goombah Frank held the purse strings. Had to be a monumental bummer for now number two "my boy."

Noodleing it around, a tic of imagination hints that Ray fancied, for Frank, a late night sons of the boot Coup de Ville

FROM THE BACK OF THE HOUSE

trunk ride . . . no not that.

Anyway, euphoric talk of one big happy family mixing like the smell of familiar in a crowded sleeping bag, Frank hired an architect, jawed over ideas with Hilda, finalized blue prints, brought in his builders (remember Frank was wired into the construction industry) and circa 1955 they began digging, cementing, bricking, and plumbing the JIM'S building. In all the dust, noise, and bang, *the* Steak House, with a *PLEASE EXCUSE OUR MESS* sign at the front door, remained open for business.

Jim's STEAK HOUSE

25

PENTHOUSE DIGS

Uncle Frank personally supervising the penthouse construction, a year later, the dust, noise and bang settled, 1800 Scranton Road had a new curb side appeal complete with a giant three-sided JIM'S neon sign on top.

Before

After

Before moving into their new digs, Aunt Hilda supervised the penthouse furnishings in the latest 1950's wall to wall plush. Frank filled in the finishing touches with (custom

FROM THE BACK OF THE HOUSE

framed and displayed on the various tapestry-covered walls) numerous original oil paintings.

Everything plugged in, hot water turned on, Hilda and Frank (Aunt Mickey too) moved to the place Les Roberts pined about in the introduction to this book: ". . . the elegant

FROM THE BACK OF THE HOUSE

apartment upstairs [above Jim's] the one boasting the most sweeping view of downtown . . . hardly a week went past that I didn't fantasize about it and yearn to one day live there. How amazing it must be to wake up every morning and look out the window at the close-by Cuyahoga River, the swooping gulls, the rush hour traffic patterns swirling around Jacobs Field, and the colorful Cleveland bridges."

Not an exaggeration, some tagged the penthouse opulence as fit for a king, at least a don. A Realtor's listing might go like this:

Hilda & Frank in new digs

Furnished Penthouse

Highlighting this crown jewel's wall to wall plush luxury is an expansive living room with white decorator fireplace and large picture window overlooking the Cuyahoga River's fabled Collision Bend. Displayed on the tapestry-covered walls are original oil paintings. Center piece here is a stunning ebony baby grand piano.

FROM THE BACK OF THE HOUSE

A step away is a quaint sun room with rattan furniture that whisks one's imagination off to soft sea breezes and tropical sunrises. Adjacent to the sun room and adding to the elegant ambiance, is a spacious dining room with polished formal walnut table and matching upholstered chairs. A creative touch is added by a restaurant styled swinging door leading to a gourmet kitchen which would steal a five-star chef's heart. Stainless wrap around counter tops, built in over/range, and dishwasher are only a few of the amenities that surround a storied country style maple kitchen table and chairs.

The plushness continues down a regal carpeted hallway where, tucked away discretely, is a modest office with oak desk and valet closet. Further along is a guest powder room with half-bath. Just beyond, two bedroom suites offer every comfort-lover's desire. Both are complete with full bath and spacious walk-in closets. Last but not least, at the end of the hall, is a gigantic laundry/utility room with storage space galore. The icing on the cake is a private outside entrance that leads to a ground-level two car attached garage.

What's not to like?!

About the bedrooms: the more modest for Aunt Mickey was furnished with a cherry bedroom set, a private bath and had double windows overlooking the Cuyahoga River. Frank and Hilda's bedroom was a Ritz suite affair with double beds, mirrored dressers, and a wide picture window with a view of JIM'S parking lot toward Scranton and Carter Roads. The bath in the master suite touted a walk in shower (a family of

FROM THE BACK OF THE HOUSE

midgets could call it home) with so many shower heads–top, front, rear, and back–like a car wash, every crack and crevasse got blitzed.

As to closets, Frank's cedar lined walk-in could pass for an uptown haberdashery: Lined up like cadets for inspection were scores of suits, sports jackets, slacks, overcoats, hats, and more shoes (spit shined) than Florsheim. Folded in cedar drawers were silk socks, boxer shorts, countless bow ties (he wore bow-tie exclusively) and, fresh from the cleaners, dozens of folded (no starch) shirts–white, white on white, variety of sports casual–all with FPM (Frank Paul Mercurio) monogrammed on the cuffs and/or breast pocket. A velvet lined jewelry case held (if melted down) at least five ingots of gold assorted cuff links.

Aunt Hilda's closet (a tad smaller with fewer of everything but not to be outdone) boasted a peephole of a window with a view of next door neighbor, Mohawk Trucking Company.

Regarding the living quarters in general, in keeping with Frank's taste, needs actually, everything (upstairs, downstairs, Ray's apartment, the garage, even the parking lot . . . well, maybe not the last two) was air conditioned.

A note about the penthouse accessibility: For Frank, Hilda, and Mickey to get to either the front-customer or backdoor kitchen entrances to JIM'S and thus in and out of the building (not to mention convenient access to *the* Steak

FROM THE BACK OF THE HOUSE

House below) necessitated a hallway to connect the old (Ray's) apartment to the new penthouse addition. Simplest solution (to Frank's direct way of thinking) was through Ray's office. Strategically located between the two apartments, the smack-in-the-middle office had been inked (with Frank's approval) in early blueprints as *HALLWAY*. No questions asked, Ray was kindly obliged to pack up and move his work space to a back bedroom (sans skylight) of the original apartment. Any wonder Ray was drinking more than usual.

For safety and not incidentally Frank's clandestine comings and goings (who knew who might be casing the joint) a second private entrance/exit had been inked into the plans. Just an arm's length from JIM'S backdoor kitchen entrance, complete with intercom wired to the upstairs, a reenforced door opened to a stairway (off/on Morse security switch just inside) that led up to Frank's gilded hideaway.

The "happy family" adventure would not be complete without mentioning automobiles. To wit, the two car garage mentioned in the above real estate ad, previously Ray's (remember Hilda didn't drive) sole domain, there was just enough room to squeeze Ray's latest Ford model from Put-in-Bay pal Bob Haulderman) in.

The squeeze evolving over the years, the garage had become dumping space for new, used, and broken JIM'S restaurant equipment, paint for the JIM'S fence, Ray's

FROM THE BACK OF THE HOUSE

barbecue grill*, and just plain junk.

No bombshell, with Uncle Frank's four-door loaded black Caddy's ** arrival, squeeze wouldn't cut it. Ray's garage junk (barbecue grill excluded) had to go as in thrown out, moved to the basement, or jammed above the garage rafters.

Frank and Caddy

Space cleared, a new electric remote control door-opener installed, there better be space enough, either side, for Frank to pull his Caddy in and gracefully egress his manly girth. If there wasn't, never mind heaven's help, not even Hilda could hide "my boy." The goombah thing everywhere, the "warm and fuzzies" had just begun.

---

* Ray loved to barbecue so there took place at JIM'S on many spring, summer and fall Sunday (JIM'S closed on the "day of rest") afternoons, a barbecue cookout. One of the reasons (actually the only reason . . . okay the

FROM THE BACK OF THE HOUSE

main reason) Ray loved a barbecue was that it took several hours to cook a good chunk of meat and in that "basting" time, Ray, along with guests, could get "basted" too.

** Every year Uncle Frank got a new Caddy from Central Cadillac. You can see it coming. Ray's pal, Bob (he sold Lincoln too), consummate salesman that he was, Frank not driving his brand, regularly nudged up and whispered in Frank's ear, "Lincoln." Finally Frank, after a month-of-Sunday's bugging by Bob, acquiesced. Shortly thereafter, negotiations began, went along, but abruptly stopped. Seems Frank blew a cork when Bob made a low ball trade-in offer for Frank's low mileage Caddy which had, "like-new-tires." After some haggling, the trade-in value of the Caddy upped, Frank agreed. A few days later, one of Frank's guys, going to pick up the new Lincoln, dropped Frank's trade-in Caddy off at Commerce Ford, drove away in Frank's new Lincoln. Shortly thereafter, Bob, looking the trade-in Caddy over, turned red, began gagging. The four "like new tires" had been replaced by four used bald ones. Bob called Ray, they met, and shared a few dozen "what are you gonna do" on the rocks.

26

HAPPY FAMILY

Ray in his cramped little removed-to-a-back-bedroom office, Uncle Frank, Aunt Hilda, and Aunt Micky settled into their plush new digs across the hallway, stress maybe is not a good word for "my boy's" condition. Ditto no wonder he drank so much. But he drank before that too. Remember what Evelyn Rose said, "He waited for a little bell to go off . . ."

One can imagine, kin folks just a hop, skip, and "yu-hoo" away, the whole thing for Ray must have seemed like continuing TV episodes of *The Twilight Zone*.

In any case, the clan adventure still in the "honeymoon" stage, another Uncle Frank hitch popped up: At breakfast, lunch, dinner, the hitch came as a complaint which resulted in a Hilda "yu-hoo" for across-the-hall Ray.

The complaint in a nut shell: Frank's new console TV was giving him fits and Aunt Hilda headaches. Seems Frank's TV picture, with gooey lines and wavy ghosts in his RCA twenty-five inch screen, resemble an uncooked Spanish omelet. A summoned TV repair person finding nothing wrong with the TV set, reported it had to be a reception problem.

Back up: In the early 50's, television the new kid on the block, hot prime time TV shows starred Ed Sullivan, Milton Berle, and Sid Caesar. These offerings, along with other popular shows– John Cameron Swasey News, *You Are There*

FROM THE BACK OF THE HOUSE

with Edward R. Murrow–were Frank staples.

Uncle Frank's TV problem, in TV-101, was this: Cable TV still a glint in Ted Turner's eyes, Satellite something in comic strips, television reception consisted entirely of *over the air* TV channels. *Over the air* TV is the free stuff that is transmitted from a TV station's antenna and picked up by a home TV via rabbit ears or outside antenna. The *over the air* signal from the TV station is what the engineers call *line of sight*. The fewer structures–trees, buildings, bridges, etcetera–in the way the better the line-of-sight reception and thus the better the TV picture was in one's living room.

You can see it coming: Frank, now down in the Flats below sea level, actually below most levels, found his TV reception of local Cleveland television stations, 3, 5, and 8 (never mind an uncooked omelet) was in Italian slang, unprintable.

Frank's whining becoming a pain in the you know where, Hilda's "yu-hoos" mounting, Raymond called a friend who had a friend and in short order there was installed a 150 foot TV

TV antenna extending (center) above JIM'S sign

FROM THE BACK OF THE HOUSE

tower/antenna atop JIM'S roof.

The TV reception not perfect but improved, Frank stopped bitching, Ray smiled, Aunt Hilda smiled, Ed Sullivan smiled, Sid Caesar smiled, everybody smiled.

While we're on TV, a word about Frank's associated television viewing snack habits. When watching his favorite shows, Aunt Hilda served Frank ice cream. He especially liked French vanilla, two scoops, with fresh Raspberries. Hilda, eager to please, served generously. If you happened to be a guest, you got some too. Some nights the topping was fresh (Frank liked most toppings as long as they were fresh) strawberries.

While we're on Frank's gastronome: A son-of-the-boot connoisseur, in love with anything food, Aunt Hilda, around 4:00 p.m., most Sundays, served up a five-course feast. This came after a Paul Bunyan breakfast–sausage, ham, bacon, pancakes, eggs, fresh fruit, coffee, toast, jelly, jam, you name it.

The Sunday main course cooked and reposing, around 3:00 p.m., Hilda would ask Ray about Saturday night business: "How'd you (she really meant "we" but she knew how to massage Ray's ego) do last night?"

Ten to fifteen thousand (remember this was the 1950s) a low-end response, Hilda would wipe a grin from her lips with both hands and gush a little, "Jessis"

Everybody smiling, Ray would haul out the Rob Roys and

FROM THE BACK OF THE HOUSE

the adults (Aunt Hilda took her insulin shot early so she could have one before wine with dinner) had a few. Underage yours truly had a "boy scout"–ginger ale with a splash of grenadine, cherry on top.

Mellowed time around 4:00 p.m., a typical two to three hour dinner might start with shrimp cocktail, soup, salad (Frank had his salad later, a goombah thing) followed by the main course which, on any given Sunday might be: pasta with red or white sauce, loin of beef, roast duck, turkey, chicken or a combination of any or all of the above. This served with an assortment of vegetables, bread butter, and wine, wine, and wine. Hilda, the grand cook, Evelyn Rose and Aunt Mickey wiped spills, stirred pots, served, and cleared the table for coffee and dessert. Of the later there were always (usually from Hough Bakeries) a variety of choices. After dessert an assortment of fruits and nuts was accompanied by cordials: B&B, Benedictine, Grand Marnier.

Throughout the meal, like King Louis times two, Frank sat at the end of the table, eating, nibbling, being served. Christmas and holidays just add three of everything above, a case of Brioschi, and Hilda's fruit cake. *

One last thing related to Frank's gastronome. Once in a while, his gout flaring up . . . you don't want to hear about wealthy men who have a bout with gout. They're like prickly pears, don't touch anywhere. Maybe a little. Frank, in his easy chair, TV set tuned on, a pillow on his ottoman, his gout

FROM THE BACK OF THE HOUSE

foot delicately rested on said pillow. White dampened-with-cold-water hanky soothing his head, Hilda, careful not to bump him anywhere, served him only one scoop of vanilla ice cream, with just one or two raspberries on top.

While we're piling on Frank, a note about his diamond "pinky rings." Acquiring a new one every few years, the diamonds progressively bigger and bigger, he bestowed the previous years' ring to his son, Frank Jr. who in turn passed on his previous ring (with Hilda's blessing) to Raymond. Over the years the diamonds had progressed to the size of a concord grape. Actually the later ones looked like a malignant growth on Frank's right pinky.

In there somewhere the ring story gets circumbobulated but the way it's told goes back to that Frank Sr./Frank Jr. cup throwing incident mentioned earlier. Seems during a meeting in Frank Sr.'s office, Frank Sr. asked Frank Jr. to get coffee for a guest (they had a full service restaurant in the basement) to which Franks Jr. replied, "Why don't you get off your fat ass and get it yourself." After a moment of awkward steeped-in-Italian-kill silence, sparks flew, a coffee cup hit the wall, and Frank Jr., not only got left out of the ring secession and a job, he got kicked out of Frank Sr.'s last will and testament forever.

So after Frank Sr.'s death (Ray had become recipient-of-the-ring since the cup throwing incident) Frank Jr. left out in the cold, his inheritance zip, he threatened to take the matter

FROM THE BACK OF THE HOUSE

to court. To avoid unpleasantry and blood, Ray offered an appeasement: Frank Jr. got the last "grape," and a few thousand in cash. Like morning mist gone by noon, visions of ugly in a Cleveland court room went away.

Years later, after Frank Jr. died, when visiting the viewing at Ripepi, the "gift grape"was missing. You assume solace for one or all of his kids (he had three). Beats the long ago Egyptian's King pyramid custom (the kings didn't take it with them) and somebody digging it up.

Anyway, for what it's worth, three of the rings were passed on to yours truly. The last about three karats (after Ray departed) was presented to yours truly by my daughter Cheri. She, it turns out, got named executrix of Ray's will (more on that later). As to the rings, I never wore any of them much, call it what you want, phoney baloney, nuts, whatever but I kept having nightmares of some goon, with a hatchet in a hurry, removing ring and finger in one fell whack. So I simply put them in a safe deposit box and, when the time came to visit Cleveland, got the latest ring out and, to keep everybody happy, slipped the bestowment on a finger. I since gave them all to wife Concetta.

So much for diamonds, gold, and you can't take it with you except for the can't take it with you. It goes like this: A few month after the move to the penthouse, Uncle Frank came home with a bill of sale for a four slot crypt (stained glass window and all), at the Knollwood Mausoleum, 1678

FROM THE BACK OF THE HOUSE

S.O.M. Center Road, Mayfield Heights.

Reason for the purchase: Frank had gone to a friend of a friend's funeral. At the grave site (April wet season in Northern Ohio) the soil Cleveland soggy, Uncle Frank (he exceeded neat freak standards by ten) seeing the casket lowered into the sogginess, had visions of himself being . . . enough said.

---

* A Christmas tradition, Hilda whipped up her special Fruit Cake and had Ray deliver (from the JIM'S liquor room) a fifth of rum which she poured over the finished cake. The cake rum-soaking took several days. One Christmas, smiling proudly, she confided she used three fifths on one cake.

27

SARASOTA, FLORIDA

Somewhere in this clan story Frank decided to retire, get out of the excavating business, sell his stake in Standard Excavating. A story floated around the clan's family tree that after Frank closed the deal (a tidy sum for his chunk of the Cleveland "hole digging" business in hand) he deposited the sizable sum in a personal bank account. Hilda, discovering the deposit slip, in the words of an eyewitness, "Aunt Hilda's stuff hit the fan." But, as always, smoothie Frank rolled things over and Hilda baked him a cake.

Back up a little, that chronological things again. When Frank talked to Tootsie about selling the Shaker House, building the penthouse above JIM'S, there was another item we're not sure he discussed with her right away or simply held it back as a surprise. The item, Sarasota, Florida.

In either case, Cleveland winters God's penalty for something not yet known, Frank looked (or had been looking) south and sure enough, there it lay: across a rickety bridge, two minutes west of Sarasota, a waterfront lot on balmy Lido Key. In case you wondered, key is dictionary defined as "a low island or reef." Lido Key is a small low island. Come to think of it, it's all an Island, one way or another.

Anyway, the lot Frank snatched up for a song (the early 50's, west coast of Florida was still orange juice stands and mosquitoes) fronted a waterway called New Pass which

FROM THE BACK OF THE HOUSE

connects Sarasota Bay to the Gulf of Mexico. On the lot he oversaw the building of a plush three bedroom fit-for-a-don retreat. *

A dock located on New Pass for Franks's Chris Craft came

FROM THE BACK OF THE HOUSE

with the package. Beyond boat is 1950s Long Boat Key. Now (2008) high rises going for about a million an inch.

Frank, Hilda, Mickey sitting on boat dock of winter digs

Welcome wagoners coming out of the Bermuda grass, friends, neighbors over for "tea," Hilda and Frank (notable Cleveland restauranteurs) made the rounds of Sarasota night life. Not unexpectedly, connections introduced from wherever, a deal was hatched by some pie in the sky Sarasota "Let's open a restaurant" wannabe. The wannabe reasoned to Frank and Hilda that a restaurant, located "Out by the Greyhound racetrack, on Tamiami Trail" would be a Fort Knox dream come true, couldn't miss.

So, gold, dreams, and bull slinging being what they are, the result was the HOLIDAY HOUSE. An evening at the HOLIDAY might include entertainment (orchestra/singer) in the main dinning room and/or, for those inclined, a banana

FROM THE BACK OF THE HOUSE

nose piano player doing imitations of Jimmy Durante, accompanied by a lady singer, in the lounge.

The fancy establishment requiring a small army of chefs, waiters, and high priced bartenders (not to mention afore noted entertainment), after six or so months in business, it didn't take a Beechwood lawyer to decipher the handwriting on the wall.

Nevertheless, as is often the case,

FROM THE BACK OF THE HOUSE

deciphering the handwriting-on-the-wall blurred by wishing, ego or both, more time passed until bottom-line reality led to the seeking of "expert advice." No surprise, heads turned north, a call was made, and in flew all around sculling expert, go-to restaurant guy from Cleveland, "my boy" Raymond.

For six days (whatever he was, Raymond knew the restaurant business better than his foreskin) he pealed back the Holiday House layer by layer, looked back, front, and up the joint. Day seven he took Tootsie and Uncle Frank aside, looked them in the eye: "Too many tits in the ringer, hands in the till, not enough Indians."

"Whata ya mean?"

"Overhead is killing you, the band, that singer, whole joint is like a stuck pig, undercooked, actually the joint is bleeding to death. Not only that, your wannabe partner's fat salaries are sucking the place dry. It's ten rats down a Flat's hole."

For sure Hilda knew when two plus two came out three and more sure Frank, surmised it was time to split. Hilda and Frank's Holiday House involvement "arrivederci," shortly thereafter the joint closed. Next chapter.

---

*Hilda, Frank, and Aunt Mickey summered in the Cleveland penthouse, wintered in the Sarasota retreat. Few years into the Florida fairy tale, Raymond up to his dog & ponypowder room tricks, Evelyn Rose threaten to leave. Hilda vowed to wade (she couldn't swim) into a Gulf sunset. Taking the threat seriously, Frank sold the Lido Key house and built another, Bayside, on Siesta Key. Sea wall, no surf.

28

IN THE MEANTIME - TWO

The Holiday House a chapter ripped out (and burned) of the JIM'S clan scrapbook, things still peachy on Ray and Evelyn Rose's side of the street, Aunt Hilda continued to preside over things domestic and business related. Frank retired, still left the apartment each day to make "appointed round" and pretty much enjoyed life. Evelyn Rose bantered about somewhere in the middle between the raisins and nuts, and Aunt Micky (regular attendee at St. Michaels on Scranton Road) prayed, lit candles, and bonded with Evelyn Rose.

As to "my boy," while dutifully managing JIM'S from his removed-to-the-back-bedroom office, a flap occurred. Seems a goombah pal of Uncle Frank had been in for dinner, got a well-done T-bone when he had ordered it medium. The overcooked meat reported to Frank, somebody (Frank, Hilda or both) said something to "my boy." That did it. Ray blew a gasket. He had cooked the goombah guy three steaks, bought him free drinks all night!

After a "the customer is always right" reminder," Ray immediately tendered his resignation, told Evelyn Rose, "Going uptown, get a job at one of the joints–Theatrical, Alpine Village, some place, any place, don't give a flying &%#."

"But Ray . . ."

Ray considering his next move (Ray was many things, but

FROM THE BACK OF THE HOUSE

most of all he knew where it was sliced, buttered, and sauteed), Aunt Hilda and Evelyn Rose cajoled (he really did have it made) pleaded, laughed, cried, he should think before making the threatened move.

After a few days brooding and a dozen or so "flying &#%'s," he sucked it up. After all, if he played this out right, one day it would all be his. He would stay but "no more goombah bull s--t."

And so, Ray stroked, the flap soothed

Ray in his office with cigar box file

(some boys have hobbies–golf, bowling, whatever–Ray's was, always open in his mind, JIM'S), he immersed himself in his "baby's" 24/7 needs.

Whether it be little side distractions–cooler on the fritz, dishwasher clogged, hot water tank leaking, toilet backed up–to more serious stuff–basement flooded (The Steak House basement at or below the Cuyahoga River level, there were several sump pumps located in shallow holes in the basement

FROM THE BACK OF THE HOUSE

floor to keep seeping river water at bay), bartenders stealing–to more mundane pains–some lady at table #6 with a draft on her neck, man at table #10 to hot, loud mouth drunk, cook sulking, and/or the "girls"bitching about splitting tips.

Amid the distractions, serious stuff, and mundane pains, Ray hunkered down in his office calculating, planning, and counting money. In between and sometimes at the same time he was on the telephone making calls to order everything from liquor to after-dinner mints. In between the out-calls he answered incoming: "Jim's Steak House, no, yes, how many, what time, got it, thank yous, nope, yep, send me a case, who? How much? NO."

Telephone technology advanced from two tin cans and a string, the JIM'S Cherry 8787 now Cherry 1-4454, same upstairs and down, when it rang (Ray ate first born if the rings exceeded three) it ding-a-linged all over the joint–Ray's office, Assistant Manager Tony's office, the bar, and the front of the house host-stand.

When Ray was out of the building, Tony answered the phone. Otherwise, a wall-phone next to the back bar, the bartender picked up the slack. Ring: "Halow, Jim's Steak House," shorter version when bar tender was busy, "Jim's Steak House, yeah."

Between calls and other stuff Ray, the go-to guy for everything from soap to mushrooms, wrote checks to vendors,

FROM THE BACK OF THE HOUSE

verified deliveries, confirmed bank deposits & withdrawals, did payroll, stacked (in neat piles) nickels, dime, quarters, pennies, singles, fives, tens, twenties, etcetera, on his desk.

When he wasn't counting money he soaked postage stamps (if they didn't have cancelled marks) off of letters for later use (this before self adhesives, he glued the stamps to envelopes) on outgoing mail.

When he wasn't busy with all of the above, he headed downstairs to nose around everything and in particular once-over: two meat and potatoes walk-in coolers, the kitchen, the back bar, and (nine of ten times) end up in the basement counting empty liquor bottles.

About the empty liquor bottles: Ray devised a flexible chute (similar to those three inch flexible tubes they use for drains) that went from the back cocktail bar down through the floor and emptied into the basement. When bartenders squeezed the last drop from a bottle of booze they sent it flying down the chute. Empties collected in a bin, every morning Ray made it to the basement where he counted empties, made a list, and ordered replacement booze.

Related to counting and booze: JIM'S liquor inventory kept in an open basement area, seems beaucoup fifths were coming up ripped off. Ray fixed it by moving the stock to a closed basement room about the size of a two-car garage. The room Ray's "holy of holies," on ceiling-high wood shelves rested Messrs. Dewars, Jack Daniels, Absolute and assorted

FROM THE BACK OF THE HOUSE

relatives from around the USA and beyond. Also present were racked (domestic and otherwise) fruits of many vines and, stacked five and six deep, cases of local and imported beer. The hooch safe behind a double locked door, the keys never left "my boy's" key ring.

While we're on booze: Ray, hating waste of any kind, while counting empty liquor bottles, selected what to the naked eye were empties–gin, scotch, bourbon, vodka, schnapps, cherry herring, whatever–and into a funneled gallon container let the "empty" bottles drain. End of a few days he had a lethal gallon of potent mix reserved for howling at the moon nights.

Yet another Ray innovation (evolved from Hilda's early penny pinching days) had to do with Aunt Hilda's advertising policy–none. The logic went, "You give 'em good food and good service, a good drink, they come back, tell people." Some call it word of mouth.

Nevertheless, Ray realizing the merits of advertising, courted advertising's twin sister, promotion. One low-cost promotion effort had Ray heading uptown to various Cleveland hotels to shell out a "few bucks" to hotel bell hops, concierges, and such while reminding them to send one and all to JIM'S. It worked and if a particular sender's name was mentioned, next time up the sender got a big tip.

Another Ray innovation (back before cell phones, email, blackberries, and mental telepathy) involved the source of many not-for-print in-house jokes–a red light. Ray had one

FROM THE BACK OF THE HOUSE

installed atop a fifty-foot poll extending above JIM'S roof. When a customer requested a cab, Ray flipped an inside switch (it worked best at night, actually only a night) and the red light glowed a signal to cab drivers that a "fare" waited at JIM'S front door.

Daytime, customer needing a cab, Ray shelled out change with a friendly, "Yellow Cab number pasted on the front of the pay phone in the lobby."

Reason for the pay phone courtesy: Outgoing calls on JIM'S business phone were verboten times ten. Handed down from James Kerkles himself, "Customer calling for a reservation, gets a busy signal, might be lost forever."

Skipping back and forth (that chronology thing again) along the "need a cab" lines, in later years Ray bought a van and offered free pickup and delivery not only to uptown hotels, but to playhouse square, and (in the 1980-90s) Jacobs Field, and Gund Arena. Customers could park at JIM'S, eat and drink, get a ride to their chosen event and be picked up after.

Aptly called *JIM'S STEAK HOUSE Courtesy Bus* (to front and back of the house people, "the van"), the designated driver was a JIM'S dishwasher (they didn't wash the van). At all hours calls came in to pick up four here, two there, a group at the somewhere. In later years it became a nightmare, but don't tell Ray.

FROM THE BACK OF THE HOUSE

"Van" at JIM'S kitchen entrance at the ready

Still another promotion service offered by Ray was a Brown's football package–tickets, booze, dinner, a deal for less than a hundred bucks a head. A boat transported participants from JIM'S to old Municipal Stadium, Monday and Sunday night games only. Some missed the boat coming back but nobody (known of) fell overboard.

Last but not least the "piece de resistance" promotion for Ray came at his all time favorite time of the year, Christmas.

Selecting a Jim's Steak House Christmas card design (the selection process, depending on the card designer's artistic proclivity, talents, gender) could take "discussions" lasting days, night, weeks. Final choice made, his signature printed (he signed early ones) inside, Ray addressed all envelopes by

FROM THE BACK OF THE HOUSE

hand, sent out thousands. A few samples from over the years:

FROM THE BACK OF THE HOUSE

And a design selected (we suspect) after a few too many "toddies for the body." An inside note accompanying this toddie's card explains it all:

JIM'S STEAK HOUSE, SKYLINE OF DOWNTOWN CLEVELAND, AS SEEN FROM OUR CRYSTAL BALL

The crystal ball was one of those basketball size glass balls you see now and then sprouting up on neighborhood front lawns.

Last but not least in the promotion department, going

Crystal Ball card

FROM THE BACK OF THE HOUSE

back forever, was the annual silver Christmas tree in the JIM'S lobby. Customers were encouraged to hang their business card on the tree. And they did. By New Years day there were hundreds of customer's cards from near and far. Ray collected the cards and sent personalized thank you notes to each and every person and/or business.

GREETING CARDS FROM AROUND THE WORLD decorate the Christmas tree in Jim's Steak House. Two of the waitreses, Miss Leona Davis and Mrs. Della Madison, examine the messages from customers who have dined at the eating place along the Cuyahoga River.

From Cleveland Press

29
JIM'S INC.

The goombah's overcooked steak incident like lost baggage on a flight to Peoria, Ray's promotions paying off, the clan was counting JIM'S cash hand over fist. So, in the best tradition of American enterprise, liability, and protecting your derriere, there came a stop, look, and listen "fork-in-the-road" for Aunt Hilda: keep the Steak House a sole (Aunt Hilda) proprietorship or incorporate.

The decision to take the Inc. turn wasn't easy. Hilda had to be convinced that it was the way to go. Remember, she and James Kerkles started this whole thing on a shoe string and a meat loaf sandwich. Hilda remembered vividly the early years at JIM'S when she cooked, washed dishes, mopped the floor, pumped the plunger, and called most of the shots. She still taped hundred dollar bills, just in case things went south, on the underside of cabinet drawers.

Most of all, she didn't want "No board of directors, stock holders, nobody" telling her what went into the "meat loaf." On and on it went until finally, accountants, lawyers, Ray, Uncle Frank, painting ugly pictures and ghastly scenarios of being sued by some green-apple-quick-step customer, Hilda signed the papers. Five shares of JIM'S stock issued, Aunt Hilda, Mrs. JIM, the Queen of the Flats (no dummy here), owned all five shares and Jim's Steak House was adopted into the Inc. world of immortal entities with Hilda as President

FROM THE BACK OF THE HOUSE

and CEO.

JIM'S now a living and breathing thing, the future looking peachy, came yet another seemingly trifle (compared to previous ones) fork in that famous road.

Years later, at the end of the "other" road, the JIM'S family found themselves staring at some long, hairy, and legless "if I had only" biting creature out of a low budget horror movie.

Briefly, the story goes like this:

From early in the 1940's (the "dekinking"of Collision Bend episode) Aunt Hilda enjoyed a warm relationship with the Carters. Remember the Carter family, the ones who had inherited the land from James Averell of the Scranton Averell Corporation connection. In short, the Carters owned the land upon which Jim's Steak House sat. The JIM'S building owned by Hilda, she operated Jim's Steak House, remodeled at her pleasure, lived upstairs, and pretty much did as she pleased. Every few years, over dinner at JIM'S, a bottle of the finest fruit of the vine, Hilda and company, breaking bread with the Carters, renewed the land lease.

Then, things to peachy to be true, like a "gotcha gush" from a vacuum packed can of fate, in around the mid 50's, due to a Carter family personal reason the heirs decided to sell their Flats' acreage, a chunk upon which sat Jim's Steak House.

A call to Hilda made, a meeting took place, and an offer looked Aunt Hilda between the eyes. In a nut shell, the

FROM THE BACK OF THE HOUSE

Carters wanted a hundred grand for the chunk of terra firma JIM'S sat on. Amid tight lips and no smiles (remember this was the time when a Cadillac Coupe De Ville was going for around four thousand and a veal cutlet dinner at Kenny King's was .75 cents) Hilda said, "Let me think about it."

Uncle Frank and Ray brought in, talk talk talk, yes, no, maybe, what-if to the nth power, the Carter's laid a second option on the table: a long term (the Carters didn't want to see JIM'S and Hilda out on the street) land lease.

More talk talk talk, maybe, nope, yep, yap, finally a bottom line–land lease, going into and beyond Y2K, was proffered.

Hilda and company thinking, "Fifty plus years in the bank, what's to lose," the lease was inked.

The plot thickens.

Before the ink was dry, the Carters eager to sell the land, came the hairy "if I had only" thing out of a two bit movie that haunts to this day. I.e., some forty years later, had the "if I had only" road been taken (Hilda and company had bought the land) this story might not be in the writing.

To wit: wind of the Carter eagerness to sell Flats' land hitting the Cleveland stratosphere, the original owners (Scranton-Averell Corporation) gobbled the acreage up like red eye gravy on a Tennessee ham and egg breakfast. Along with the "ham"went the whole hog, the JIM'S land lease included.

FROM THE BACK OF THE HOUSE

New landlords announced, the Scranton-Averell purchase bugled around town, Hilda and company (fifty year lease in hand) yawned a "so what."

"Ooops.'

Turns out the "so what" was a ton of "that's what."

Namely, in the 1980s, the Scranton-Averell corporation formed a partnership with Forest City called the Scranton Development Company. * Suddenly the land beneath Jim's Steak House, foundation and all, became shifting sand.

Maybe that's why they call it real estate. What's real?

In short, location location location. Who could have known in the 1950's that all that Flats' land would be worth a hill of beans, let alone the gleam in some boss hog's eye. The gleam's source, a dream to build (across the Cuyahoga River from a proposed Cleveland something or other Convention center) town houses, apartments,

FROM THE BACK OF THE HOUSE

and quaint little shops on the peninsula where JIM'S sat. All of it connected by (for conventioneers attending conventions in the new tax payer paid convention center) a pedestrian walkway across the Cuyahoga. Boss hog's grand development scheme is suggested in a plan envisioned by a Cleveland developer that appeared in a Plain Dealer story circa 1960.

Reproduced here, note that JIM'S is/was located about where the Marina (bottom center) basin is proposed.

A million here a billion there . . . when you're talking tax payer billions, is like some pot luck war in "over there" and the generals, smoking cigars and sipping Jack Daniels, calculate "collateral damage." Like somebody once wrote, "Bombs from the sky is like the Fourth of July, bombs from a bus is different stuff."

Anyway, turns out the long term lease Hilda inked would not only come back to bite, the horror movie was a hairy double feature.

To wit: in the late 1980s, things at JIM'S were tighter than skin on Bonnie Lou's sixth face lift. To ease the negative cash flow, Ray Rockey, to get a lower monthly payment, renegotiated the JIM'S lease giving back years to Forest City. Ray Rockey gone to his reward January 1995, the land lease expired 31 December 1996, one wonders (if an after-life is so) what impact the renegotiated expiration date is having on Ray's "other side" repose.

For what it's worth, as of this writing (2008) the land sits

FROM THE BACK OF THE HOUSE

undeveloped pretty much the way it was in 1996. JIM'S closed for ten plus years, the empty JIM'S building where once so much living, laughing, and love took place looks like a ghost lost between time. More on that later.

In any case, skipping back, the lease signed, things at JIM'S hunky-dory, one hot July afternoon in 1957, they delivered the Cleveland Press to JIM'S front door. Imagine the *Second Coming* and the *Big Bang* all in one. Suffice it to say, the "power of the press" had new meaning. Next chapter.

---

* In 1921 the Ratowczer (later changed to Ratner) family founded Forest City which began as a lumber materials company. Soothsayers aside, wouldn't it be Indian-ghost ironic that the original JIM'S was relocated to the Lumbermen's Club in the Flats which had been a clubhouse for lumber barons which was later raised for the "dekinking"of Collusion Bend and, still later the land ended up owned by Forest City which started out as a lumber company? Considering the way the land lease for JIM'S turned out, and where lumber comes from, it give new meaning to Kilmer's "as lovely as a tree." That or all the ghosts stories about the Jim's building are true!

30
POWER OF THE PRESS
1957

The JIM'S land lease tucked away for future "what-ifs," television news the new kid on the block, local newspapers enjoyed (in the hearts of moms, pops, and kids who could read) big dog status. Even now, fifty years later, there's something about seeing your name in print. It's a riveting power that changes lives, worlds, appetites, eating, drinking habits, and that too.

Along those lines, in particular is the power of the "press" riveting to the owners of public establishments. Especially riveted is print to owners of eating establishments who are razor-blade skittish about impressions (food or otherwise) that might get dumped into hungry patrons' minds.

So you can imagine, the JIM'S brain trust's riveting interest when up popped (Jim's Steak House plastered all over it) a Cleveland Press article by none other than that bon vivant about town restaurant critiquer, Winsor French.

A quick rewind: remember Winsor's thief in the night, slap in the face, "reach out and grab it" article that appeared in the Cleveland Press, August, '52? In part, this one:

> Jim's Steak House on Collision Bend in the Flats . . . could easily become one of the most exciting and spectacular restaurants in the country. If, that is, someone would only use a

FROM THE BACK OF THE HOUSE

> little inexpensive imagination . . . How anyone could turn their back on such fantasy is beyond the limits of my understanding. A reasonably small sum of money could transform the restaurant in nothing flat to something every bit as startling as the famous Rivera high above the Hudson in Manhattan, or even the Top of the Mark in San Francisco . . . The beauty and the magic are there all right, someone only has to reach out and grab it.

Remember the aftermath, around the kitchen table of the Shaker Heights kitchen: Hilda, Frank, and Ray sitting in stoic silence, the Winsor rebuff like the layered smell of rendering animal fat slaking the JIM'S air . . . well, five years later, Aunt Hilda's "hayseed critic with a wild hair up his nose" was at it again.

Blow by blow it went like this: Sweltering Monday afternoon of July 29, 1957, Hilda, Frank, and Ray, this time sitting around the kitchen table of the Penthouse above JIM'S, read and reread an all new Restaurant Row column by French. There it was, for all Cleveland and the world to see, a second slap in the face from French. The grim faced trio read it again:

> Every time I pass Jim's Steak House down in the Flats at Collision Bend I am plunged into despair. This, surely, is the town's most romantic and exciting location for a restaurant, regardless of the season.
> Even in winter when the river traffic no longer

FROM THE BACK OF THE HOUSE

> flows past the willows seeping over the embankment you have the skyline, the draw bridges jumping across the twisting river and the angular elevators to help impress you that this is quite a city.
> The Steak House, of course, should make an all out effort to dramatize its unique location. There should be a broad terrace where patrons could sit on mile summer evenings over cocktails, watching the freighters navigate the bend.
> Large windows ought to frame the spectacular outlook and the restaurant itself should be incidental to its surroundings.
> So what has been done about it? Nothing at all, naturally. Dark awnings screen the windows that are too small and too highly placed to see out of properly and still another wall has been surfaced with opaque, glass brick!
> If this were San Francisco the place would be a sort of grounded Top of the Mark, sightseeing busses would crowd the parking lot and the bar would be a Mecca for camera-carrying tourists. But what a lost cause it all is. (Cleveland Press, July 29, 1957)

For those over age fifty imagine the JIM'S brain trust reading and rereading this latest blast from French. Now imagine what it must have been like in FDR's inner circle the afternoon of December 7, 1941. For those under fifty imagine the Clinton bedroom the day after the Monica Lewinsky story broke.

FROM THE BACK OF THE HOUSE

Something like that.

Two pictures of a thousand words shows what French was writing about:

Main dining room, Carter room to left behind glass block

Bar and lounge

FROM THE BACK OF THE HOUSE

Anyway, the JIM'S brain trust, coffee spiked with shots of 100 proof something, expletives deleted, shortly thereafter retained architect William Ianne who (pretty much based on Winsor's guidelines) came up with a grand design and the Winsoring renaissance of Jim's Steak House began.

31

The New Jim's

In the spring of 1958 the new JIM'S was begun–excavating, pouring concrete, plumbing, windowing, hammering, painting, carpeting–and in it all JIM's again remained open with a sign in the lobby: PLEASE EXCUSE OUR MESS, REMODELING TO SERVE YOU BETTER - THANK YOU FOR YOUR PATIENCE, signed Raymond Rockey Mgr.

Some months later, the grand opening of the Seaway Room (the Seaway designation never caught on, don't ever recall hearing, "I wish to be seated in the Seaway Room") premiered.

Designed by William Ianne, built by Schirmer-Peterson Co., and decorated by Aunt Hilda, the new (around $140,000) Jim's Steak House greeted the Cleveland dining world.

FROM THE BACK OF THE HOUSE

Artist Stephen Knapp captured the ambiance in water color.

PAINTING BY STEPHEN KNAPP

Jim's Steak House

Knapps's painting featured JIM'S along with other establishments throughout the U.S., (one being the Mayflower Hotel, Washington D.C.) in *The New Ford Treasury of Favorite Recipes* book. The Knapp painting caption read:

> JIM'S STEAK HOUSE, specializing in prime steaks, is located at 1800 Scranton Road in Cleveland, Ohio. The glass-walled dining room affords diners a magnificent view of lake freighters navigating Collision Bend on their way to steel mills and limestone docks. Lunch and dinner served weekdays. Closed Sundays and holidays. Reservations necessary.

In short, gone were the dark awnings and glass block that

FROM THE BACK OF THE HOUSE

Winsor French abhorred. Now, through massive windows stretching floor to ceiling, diners ooed and awed the sweeping views of Cleveland's skyline, the picturesque Cuyahoga meandering around Collision Bend, and football field size oar boats gliding by. Gone too was, now covered with plush wall to wall pastel carpeting, the parquet wood floors.

In the evening, lighting turned low by Raymond–table candles flickering, sparkling white tablecloths and napkins, spotless silverware, river shimmering reflected lights of the Terminal Tower–JIM'S inspired more juices than gastric.

The words of the bon vivant man about town who started it all, Winsor French, pretty much nails it:

JIM'S Steak house down there on Collision Bend in the Flats, after weeks and weeks of invasions by contractors, carpenters, interior decorators and so on, has finally emerged from the dusty chaos and is surely one of the most spectacular restaurants in the country.

Regardless of how celebrated the steaks may be that emerge from Frank and Hilda Mercurio's kitchens, nothing, absolutely nothing matters here but the view and you have never seen anything like it.

The walls now are great sheets of Thermopane

185

FROM THE BACK OF THE HOUSE

glass that look out across the lawn falling down to the river, and beyond at the towering background of the city. Thousands upon thousands of lights sparkle in the night like so many jewels flung against the sky and even now boats come and go, disturbing the quiet reflections winking back from the dark sheen of the twisting river.

It is as if you stepped into a fabulous fantasy of lights and shadows and curious movements. Cars dart back and forth across the bridges like illuminated toys, lights go on and off in high offices as charwomen go about their nightly business and the jagged and towering skyline becomes a fantastic mirage, gaudy as a painted theatrical backdrop (Told you this was Ray's stage). Hackneyed as the phrase may be, breathtaking I am afraid, is the only description for all this.

Bringing all this dazzling drama into the famous old restaurant cost the trifling sum of $140,000 but it would still be worth it at double the price. How the waitresses, the Mercurios, Mrs. Jim and Frank, son and daughter-in-law, Ray and Evelyn Rockey, manage to keep their minds on the business of the day, however, I can't imagine.

And as to that, perhaps I should mention that as far as they are all concerned the view is merely incidental. They still continue to serve over a ton of steaks a week, garnished with the usual vegetables, including some of the most searing hot relishes I have ever tasted.

There is a fine bar too. Which also shares the view and right at the moment the family is

FROM THE BACK OF THE HOUSE

considering a pianist.

Well there it is. The Flats have always been the most dramatic corner of Cleveland and for years Jim's Steak House has been in the middle of it behind stubbornly drawn curtains.

And rather selfishly when you consider the Mercurios and Rockeys live upstairs in a penthouse enjoying the same panorama. But forgive them. The wrong has been corrected with gestures. (Cleveland Press 1959)

Not bad, bring out the Rob Roys!

Another noted publication, the Diners Club (the mother of credit cards) monthly magazine's (June, 1959) cover consisted of matchbook covers of Cleveland's then famous joints: The Purple Tree (in the Manger Hotel), the Sheraton Cleveland, The Playhouse, Blue Grass, Broglio's, The Roman Gardens,

FROM THE BACK OF THE HOUSE

Greenbrier, Hollenden House, Luccioni's, Little Ted's and right there, smack middle left, guess who.

Inside, JIM'S got top-of-the-page billing, with a photo of a couple seated at a window side table, under the banner *TheStory of Cleveland* the caption: "JIM's Steak House,

JIM'S STEAK HOUSE. Romantically located on the Cuyahoga River which winds through Cleveland like a corkscrew, Jim's lets diners get a view of Cleveland's skyline both night and day.

Romantically located on the Cuyahoga River which winds through Cleveland like a corkscrew, Jim's lets diners get a view of Cleveland's skyline both night and day."

With all this "ink" you can imagine, things looking up up

FROM THE BACK OF THE HOUSE

up for JIM'S, Aunt Hilda basked in the glow of a feature story by Gus Utter * :

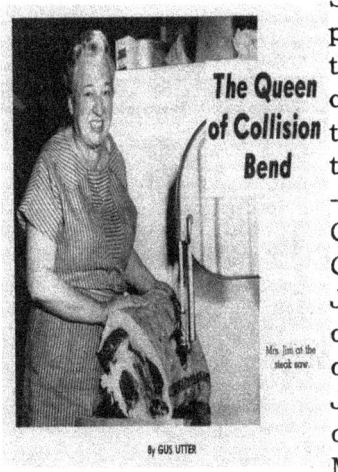

The Queen of Collision Bend

Hilda at the JIM'S meat saw

Scientists are orderly people who like to classify things, so it should be called to their attention that this may be termed the Geo-Gastronomical year at Collision Bend in the Cuyahoga River where Jim's Steak House is observing nearly a third of a century with Mrs. Jim officiating in one role or another.

Mrs. Jim is known by no other name to a multitude of local customers and visitors from abroad. In fact, says Mrs. Jim, her epitaph likely will be inscribed that way, instead of with her legal name: Mrs. Hilda Mercurio. Epitaph writers need not reach for their chisels, however, because Mrs. Jim, at 61 and standing 5 feet 11 inches, carries a proud 200 pounds with the easy maneuverability of an ore carrier in ballast and she has every intention of surviving for many years. Ore carriers and other river traffic provide a background for the Collision Bend steak house and pass within a biscuit toss of the quiet dining room, wide windows and graceful lawn adorned by unobtrusive shade trees.

Mrs. JIM'S establishment is probably the only

FROM THE BACK OF THE HOUSE

eatery in the world where customers may be dazzled by a steamer's searchlight because a lake skipper often aims a beam into the dining room by way of greeting as they pass.
There are other things unique about Jim's Steak House, named for Jim Kerkles, a first husband and cofounder with Hilda, who died 21 years ago. Mrs. Jim and her manager, Raymond Rockey, son of her late sister, serve only such manly provender as steak, ham, lamb chops and the like, and trout or other fish on special days.

Hoopla, glitz, restaurant fame, special days indeed. Like a country and western singer suddenly discovered by big city struts, heart on sleeve, soul in the past, thrust naked into a new world of candle light kneesies-under-the-table, JIM'S had arrived at Uptown Hall center stage.

Alas, some envisioned JIM'S had become like one of those pouched-trout-in-lemon sauce-on-a-bed-of-dill "fine dining" restaurant.

Close but no cigar. JIM'S setting had changed but Cleveland's meat and potato spot had not. In short, the food remained the same, the "girls" in white uniforms remained the same, the excellent service remained the same, the bar, the Carter Room, the cooks, bartenders, scullers, and assistant manager Tony, remained the same.

Even Ray Rockey, going about his appointed day to day routine, remained the same . . . almost. Almost because Ray,

FROM THE BACK OF THE HOUSE

now up to his neck in heady Uptown Hall panache, found more restaurant groupies bouncing off the ceiling than bubbles in a just opened bottle of Asti Spumonti. The genteel Mrs., Ms., and Misses, in and out of the powder room (more willing, more giving, more taking, more aggressive, just plain more) steamed up the windows and fuzzed up "my boys" focus.

Ray fuzzed up in overdrive, a little more than six years into his marriage to Evelyn Rose, he announced to her (about his latest amour–a JIM'S "girl") a vexing concern: "If she's pregnant I want a divorce."

"My boy" intended to marry the madam and save another little one from the bastard pile of who, what, where, and when. Evelyn Rose informed him, "They'll laugh you out of court."

Turns out the JIM'S "girl" was "oops" tubular or just plain late, and the shine on another make-believe bugger brought again into question Ray's squiggles (that Navy radar school thing).

Never mind the handwriting on the wall, six years after the two-bit "I do's," canned confetti, and faux whatever, the marriage of Raymond and Evelyn Rose was D.O.A..

A final nail in the "until death do us part" driven, Evelyn Rose began taking cosmetology classes. Her address still 1800 Scranton Road, she and Ray slept in separate bedrooms. Across the hall in the penthouse, "my boy" up to

FROM THE BACK OF THE HOUSE

his old dog and pony tricks, Aunt Hilda said novenas, Aunt Mickey lit more candles at Saint Michaels, and Uncle Frank visited friends. And like they always did, *The* Steak House "help" continued cranking it out with one exception–now they tiptoed around like upstairs slept the gorilla ghost of Christmas past.

During this time, "my boys" libido gone wild, JIM'S booze lists (written and edited by Raymond) blossomed in leaps and bounds. From an early menu's "Around-The-World" selections a few notables: *Rose-I-Love, Honeymoon, Sugar House, Angel's Tit, Clover Club, Between Sheets* . . . take a look. First a couple close-ups then the whole nine yards.

Jim's Steak House
DRINK LIST

PUNCHES — SMASHES — COLLINSES — RICKEYS — DAISIES — FIZZES — TODDIES
SOURS — COBBLERS — FLIPS — PICK-ME-UPS — AFTER-DINNER DRINKS

COCKTAILS — MIXED DRINKS . . . Around-The-World Selection

Jim's Special .75	Side Car .75	Bishop .65	Tom Collins .60
Martini .60	Stinger .75	Missouri Lil .75	John Collins .60
Extra Dry Martini .75	Pink Lady .75	Big Head Mary .75	Frisco Collins .75
Vodka Martini .75	Grasshopper .75	Pale Moon .75	Cuba Libre .65
Manhattan .60	Flying Hopper .85	Shark's Tooth 1.25	Gin and Tonic .70
Orange Blossom .75	Pink Squirrel .75	King Peg 1.25	Puerto Rico .65
Rob Roy .85	Sky Ride .75	Champagne 1.25	Claret Cobbler .85
Dubonnet .65	Old Fashioned .60	Frozen Daiquiri .85	Screwdriver .75
Perfect .60	Sazerac .75	Queen of Fizzes .85	Gin Daisy .70
Gibson .60	Hunters .75	Planter's Punch .85	Gin Buck .60
Alexander .75	Clover Club .75	Singapore Sling 1.00	Gin Rickey .60
Bacardi .65	April Dream .75	Shanghai Sling 1.00	Hot or Cold Toddy .75
Jack Rose .75	Star .65	Suissess .85	Sherry Flip .75
Daiquiri .65	Coffee .75	New Orleans Fizz .85	Milk Punch .85
Brandy .75	Honolulu .75	North Pole 1.00	Egg Nog .75
Bronx .60	Palm Leaf .75	Tropic Julep 1.00	Mint Julep 1.00
Rose-I-Love .75	Ward Eight .75	Toddy Smash .75	Mary 1.00
Bachelor .75	Panama .75	Whiskey Sour .60	Gimlets .75
Japonic .75	Carribbean Punch 1.00	Drake .75	Between Sheets 1.00
Honeymoon 1.00	Eclipse .75	Ship To Shore 1.00	Sugar House .75

WINES AND LIQUOR

Apricot Delight 1.00	Dubonnet .75	
Alexander .75	Bronx .75	
Bacardi .60	Hunters .65	
Brandy Cocktail .60	Jack Rose .85	
Clover Club .60	Manhattan .75	
Champagne Cocktail .75	Martini 1.00	

Daiquiri Cocktail .65

Old Fashioned .60
Orange Blossom .80
Scarlet O'Hara .75
Side Car .75
Stinger .75

Sloe Gin Fizz .60	Sherry Flip .65	Cuban Libre .55
Silver Fizz .60	Whiskey Sour .75	Planters Punch .75
Golden Fizz .60	Brandy Sour .75	Angel's Tit .80
Royal Fizz .60	John Collins .75	Creme de Menthe Frappe
New Orleans Fizz .75	Singapore Gin Sling .75	(Green or White) .60
Porto Rican Rickey .60	Gin Daisy .60	

FROM THE BACK OF THE HOUSE

Jim's Steak House
DRINK LIST

PUNCHES — SMASHES — COLLINSES — RICKEYS — DAISIES — FIZZES — TODDIES
SOURS — COBBLERS — FLIPS — PICK-ME-UPS — AFTER-DINNER DRINKS

COCKTAILS — MIXED DRINKS . . . Around-The-World Selection

Jim's Special	.75	Side Car	.75	Bishop	.65	Tom Collins	.60
Martini	.60	Stinger	.75	Missouri Lil.	.75	John Collins	.60
Extra Dry Martini	.75	Pink Lady	.75	Big Head Mary	.75	Frisco Collins	.75
Vodka Martini	.75	Grasshopper	.75	Pale Moon	.75	Cuba Libre	.65
Manhattan	.60	Flying Hopper	.85	Shark's Tooth	1.25	Gin and Tonic	.70
Orange Blossom	.75	Pink Squirrel	.75	King Peg	1.25	Puerto Rico	.65
Rob Roy	.85	Sky Ride	.75	Champagne	1.25	Claret Cobbler	.85
Dubonnet	.65	Old Fashioned	.60	Frozen Daiquiri	.85	Screwdriver	.75
Perfect	.60	Sazerac	.75	Queen of Fizzes	.85	Gin Daisy	.70
Gibson	.60	Hunters	.75	Planter's Punch	.95	Gin Buck	.60
Alexander	.75	Clover Club	.75	Singapore Sling	1.00	Gin Rickey	.60
Bacardi	.65	April Dream	.75	Shanghai Sling	1.00	Hot or Cold Toddy	.75
Jack Rose	.75	Star	.65	Suissess	.85	Sherry Flip	.75
Daiquiri	.65	Coffee	.75	New Orleans Fizz	.85	Milk Punch	.85
Brandy	.75	Honolulu	.75	North Pole	1.00	Egg Nog	.75
Bronx	.60	Palm Leaf	.75	Tropic Julep	1.00	Mint Julep	1.00
Rose-I-Love	.75	Ward Eight	.75	Toddy Smash	.75	Mazy	1.00
Bachelor	.75	Panama	.75	Whiskey Sour	.60	Gimlets	.75
Japonic	.75	Carribbean Punch	1.00	Drake	1.00	Between Sheets	1.00
Honeymoon	1.00	Eclipse	.75	Ship To Shore	1.00	Sugar House	.75

HIGHBALLS

Bonded Rye and Bourbon		Scotch		Scotch		Canadian	
Old Overholt	.75	Dewar's White Label	.65	Grant's	.75	Canadian Club	.55
Bonded Bourbon	.75	Old Smuggler	.65	Ballantine's 17-year	1.25	Seagram's V-O	.55
Old Forester	.75	Teacher's	.65	Bell's 20-year	1.25	MacNaughton's	.55
Old Grand Dad	.75	Black and White	.65	Johnny Walker Blk	.75	John Jameson	.65
Old Fitzgerald	.75	Cuttysark	.75	Johnny Walker Red	.65	Bushmills	.65
Old Taylor	.75	Ballantine	.75	Haig & Haig Pinch	.75	**Vodka**	
Old Crow	.65	White Horse	.65	Haig & Haig 5 Star	.65	Smirnoff	.55
Kentucky Tavern	.75	King's Ransom	.75	Grand MacNish	.65	Reiska	.55
I. W. Harper	.75	Chivas Regal	.75	Martin's V-O	.75		

STRAIGHT AND BLENDED WHISKIES

Ancient Age	.50	Echo Springs	.50	Seagram's 7-Crown	.45	Hunter's	.45
Glenmore	.50	Barclay	.50	Calvert's Reserve	.45	Schenley	.45
Early Times	.50	Walker's Deluxe	.50	Lord Calvert's	.50	Imperial	.45

Cognacs		Rums		Gins			
Remy Martin	.85	Bacardi Silver Label	.55	House of Lords	.75		
Courviesier	.75	Bacardi Gold Label	.65	Beefeaters'	.75		
Hennessy 3-Star	.75	Carioca Gold Label	.50	Booth's	.75		
Martell 3-Star	.75	Jamaica Red Heart	.75	Gordon's	.50		
Christian Bros.	.60	Meyers	.75	Sloe Gin	.60		
Applejack	.60	Carioca	.50				

Cordials				Beer, Ales and Stouts			
Chartreuse	.75	Grand Marnier	.75	Gold Bond	.25	Labatt's Bass Pale	.45
Creme de Cacao	.75	Creme de Menthe		Budweiser	.35	Standard	.25
Apricot Brandy	.75	Frappe	.75	Carling's	.30	Miller's	.35
Cherry Brandy	.75	Benedictine	.75	Heineken's Lager	.65	Guinness	.50
Cherry Heering	.75	B and B	.75	P. O. C.	.25	Lowenbrau	.75
Cointreau	.75	Anisette	.75	Schlitz	.35	Blue Ribbon	.35
Gilka Kummel	.75	Curacao	.75				
Angel's Kiss	.75	King Alfonso	.75				
Drambuie	.75	Irish Mist	.75				
Charley-Rose	.85	Irish Coffee	.85				

FROM THE BACK OF THE HOUSE

WINES AND LIQUORS

CKTAILS
int Julep	1.00	Apricot Delight	.75	Dubonnet	.60	Rob Roy .8!
om & Jerry	.75	Alexander	.75	Bronx	.60	Old Fashioned .6(
old Toddy	.60	Bacardi	.65	Hunters	.75	Orange Blossom .6(
ot Toddy	.60	Brandy Cocktail	.65	Jack Rose	.65	Scarlet O'Hara .7!
orses Neck	.60	Clover Club	.75	Manhattan	.60	Side Car .7!
nk Lady	.75	Champagne Cocktail	1.00	Martini	.60	Stinger .7!
		Daiquiri Cocktail	.65			

ORTED DRINKS
om Collins	.80	Sloe Gin Fizz	.65	Sherry Flip	.65	Cuban Libra .5!
in Fizz	.60	Silver Fizz	.75	Whiskey Sour	.80	Planters Punch .7!
in Buck	.60	Golden Fizz	.75	Brandy Sour	.75	Angel's Tit .8(
in Rickey	.60	Royal Fizz	.75	John Collins	.00	Creme de Menthe Frappe,
oe Gin Rickey	.60	New Orleans Fizz	.75	Singapore Gin Sling	.75	(Green or White) .6(
		Porto Rican Rickey	.80	Gin Daisy	.80	

MESTIC CORDIALS — IMPORTED CORDIALS
	Pony		Pony		Pony		Pony
aristine	.60	Curacao	.50	Creme de Cacao	.80	B & B	.7!
lackberry	.60	Kuemmel	.50	Creme de Menthe, green or white	.80	V. C. Vieille Cure	.7!
ach	.75	Triple Sec	.60	Cointreau	.75	Benedictine	.7!
herry	.75	Anisette	.60	Drambuie	.75	Kahlua (Licor de Cafe)	.6(
outhern Comfort		Drink	.60	Bock & Rye Drink	.50	C & B	.8(
				Grand Marnier	.85		

ORTED SCOTCH AND IRISH WHISKEY
achers	.65	Johnny Walker, Red Label	.65	King's Ransome	
at 69	.65	Johnny Walker, Black Label	.75	Ballantine's	.7!
artin's V. V. O.	.65	Haig & Haig, 5 Star	.65	Cutty Sark	.7!
ack & White	.65	Haig & Haig, Pinch Bottle	.75	Dewar's White Label	.6!
	White Horse	.65	John Jameson & Son (Irish Whiskey)	.85	

MESTIC BRANDIES — IMPORTED BRANDIES
ildick's Applejack Drink	.80	Leroux	.60	Martell Cognac, 3 Star	.7!
he Christian Brothers	.60	Hennessy Cognac, 3 Star	.75	Remy Martin	.8!
	Merito	.70	Metaxa	.85	

ORTED RUM
acardi, Silver Label	.50	Marimba Rum	.45	Red Heart Jamaica Rum	.75
acardi, Gold Label	.65	Carioca Rum, Gold Label	.45	Meyer's Jamaica Rum	.75
		Carioca Rum, White Label	.45		

SLOE GIN
ordon's	.50	Fleischmann's	.50	Seagram's Ancient	.45	John Collins .40 Leroux .5(

R AND ALE — 25c

BLACK HORSE ALE Imported Btl. .40¢

ERICAN AND CANADIAN WHISKIES
ld Oscar Pepper	.40	Weideman's 31	.50	Seagram's 5 Crown	.40	Kentucky Tavern .7!
henley	.40	Imperial	.40	Seagram's 7 Crown	.45	Old Crow .7!
rul Jones	.40	Bond & Lilliard	.40	Four Roses, Blend	.45	Canadian Club .5!
M. De Luxe	.40	Park & Tilford, Reserve	.40	Four Roses, Straight	.50	Harwood's .6(
alvert's Special	.40	Park & Tilford, Private		Hunter's	.45	Seagram's V. O. .5!
alvert's Reserve	.45	Stock	.50	Old Granddad	.75	Lord Calvert's .5(
olden Wedding	.45	Mount Vernon Rye	.50	Old Taylor	.75	Old Overholt Rye .7!
		Old Forester	.75			

ORTED and DOMESTIC CHAMPAGNE and SPARKLING WINES
umm's, Extra Dry	13.00	Fountain Grove	6.50	Dry Imperator	6.5(
arles Heidsieck	13.00	Sparkling Mosselle	Pint 3.25	St. Remy	4/5 Pint 3.25

ORTED WINES
rt, Sherry Brilliante	6.00	Chianti	Pint 3.25	Dubonnet 5.00
		Glass	.80	

MESTIC WINES
	Bottle	Glass		Bottle	Glass		Bottle	Glass
uterne (Haute or Dry)	3.50	.40	Claret	3.50	.40	Muscatel	3.50	.40
rginia Dare	3.50	.40	Tokay	3.50	.40	Dry Sherry	3.50	.40
rt	3.50	.40	Sherry	3.50	.40	Blackberry	3.50	.40

And to think, no "parental discretion" advisory!

---

* As noted previously, ditto for the publication of writer Gus Utter

PART III

PORTENTS

HARBINGER

Jim's Steak House arrived at "big time and strut," Ray Rockey's center stage gait more cocky than John Wayne on a good day, 1959, the 13th of June, one of those Cleveland only thunderstorms (a harbinger of more ominous things to come) blew in across Lake Erie and cold-cocked one of Aunt Hilda's (planted-from-sapling on JIM'S front lawn) prize willow trees. Discovering the damage, Aunt Hilda called a tree doctor. Doctor arrived, willow still living, doc propped it upright, secured it with steel cables, and gave it a shot of "tree hemoglobin." After Aunt Mickey

Mrs. Frank P. Mercurio and Sick Tree

FROM THE BACK OF THE HOUSE

blessed it, Hilda and tree posed for The Plain Dealer. The PD story:

> Storm-Damaged Willow in Flats Saved from Death
> A tree grows in The Flats
> It is a willow planted 19 years ago at 1800 Scranton Road S.W. by Mrs. Frank P. Mercurio, owner of Jim's Steak House. Five weeks ago a storm uprooted, broke and bruised the tree.
> "Mrs. Jim," as everybody calls her, summoned a tree surgeon. The tree was bandaged, set back in place, and propped by nine steel cables.
> 'It is still a sick tree,' she said yesterday, 'but it is living and by next year will be in good shape again.'
> The tree restoration job costs $600 but Mrs Jim considers it well worth it. She likes to keep the patch of lawn on the Cuyahoga River green and decorated with flowering plants.
> She began in the restaurant business in 1922 with her fist husband, the late Jim Kerkles and has had a place in the flats since 1930. (P.D., June 13, 1959)

The willow taking hold, living to shade yet another JIM'S lunch bunch, turns out the harbinger thing would turn out to be more than an old wives tale. More later.

33

SHEEPSKIN

Aunt Hilda's willow doing fine, the harbinger-thing in waiting, in the fall of 1959 there came to the fore of clan discussions talk about sheep skin as in a college degree. Namely, getting one with the "getting one" directed at yours truly.

It should be noted, as far as the clan was concerned, it didn't matter how, or in what field one got a sheep skin (none of the clan had one) just get one.

Along those line, for some reason, even now, there is some mystique surrounding "getting a sheep skin." I think it has to do with acquiring things, place at the table, rank and all that etcetera stuff that gurus say isn't important but what do they know. Look where we are today.

In any case, from early on yours truly dabbling in ego (high school plays, Cain Park summer theater), in some cockeyed way the clan's sheep skin edict coming to pass, I landed in Pittsburgh, a freshman in Carnegie Mellon's Drama Department.

Second semester, into play acting, real life stuff barged onto the JIM'S stage. It goes like this: Ray telephoned me to say he had a friend whose daughter had been bitten by wannabe as in "I wanna be a star, actress, leading lady."Ray went on: daughter and her mother (Charlotte) were coming to Pittsburgh, would I (without the question mark) give them a

FROM THE BACK OF THE HOUSE

guided tour of the Carnegie campus, show the ropes, you know.

"Sure."

Soon thereafter I rendezvoused for dinner with Charlotte and daughter at a swanky Pittsburgh hotel. Charlotte turned out to be a shapely women, 5' 6", brunette, brown inquisitive eyes. Daughter smiled a lot. Dinner nice, afterward we took a tour of the Carnegie campus, thank you and good night.

Not making much of it at the time, too busy with other things. One, two, and three of the "other things" turned out (after a brief encounter at the irresistible Y of pleasure that resulted in marriage to a local Pennsylvanian, Patricia McCormick) to be a long and gnarled story.

You can fill in the obvious but a child on the way, now a family man ("Everybody" knowing that a family and a career in the theater is like fleas getting dogs), Ray presented me with a collection of colorful brochures touting various college restaurant programs. The one offered at Michigan State's Kellogg Hotel and Restaurant Management school, got the nod.

The plan being: no more play acting, get a degree in restaurant management and follow, in the Jim's Steak House tradition, Ray.

Long story short, off to East Lansing, wife Patricia stayed behind shuttling between Cleveland and her folks in Pennsylvania. Daughter Cheri born 11 December 1960, yours

FROM THE BACK OF THE HOUSE

truly commuting from East Lansing, Cheri and her mother spent a lot of time living with the clan above JIM'S. Cheri, the only baby (besides *the* Steak House) that Ray had ever known, became the apple of his eye. To Cheri, Ray became "Papa."

The clan intrigue evolving, yours truly and Michigan State's restaurant management program mixing like then and never, after a short talk with an academic advisor, she suggested switching major to something more in tune with a theater background. A "why not" resulted in transferring to something (it was 1960) called TV&Radio.

College major changed, the sheep skin imperative (in my mind, sheepskin is a sheepskin, right? Wrong!) taken care of, somehow Ray didn't get told of the switch.

Eventually (three years later via a food broker friend of Rays attending a restaurant convention) the switch in college majors got back to Cleveland, stuff hit the fan, and therein might lie a tick of motivation for Ray Rockey's last will and testament. Simply put, the episode might have influenced his decision (a Ray Rockey gotcha thing, more later) to scratch yours truly from his will.

Whatever and enough said. Maybe one thing. When you play gotcha in the game of life, be sure it's what you want because when the game is over there's no allie allie in free and who does what on whose grave is serious stuff.

34

WIND FROM BRISTOL

In the meantime, that wind back in June of '59 that toppled Aunt Hilda's willow tree, the harbinger of more ominous things to come . . . turns out it was just that but this time the gust was southerly, blowing in from down around Bristol, Virginia, a Category 5 dubbed Charlotte. The very one yours truly had had a whiff of (at Ray's request, the tour for her and daughter) when attending Carnegie Mellon.

Charlotte

As to 1800 Scranton Road, some say Charlotte blew into JIM'S powder room unannounced. Others say Ray met her at the JIM'S bar. Whatever, Ray Rockey picked up the prevailing winds and Charlotte ended up on his list of validating things to do.

Judging by how things later turned out, some suggested it was Charlotte who was doing the validating.

In any case, turns out Ray was double (double is a relative word) dipping all along. Also turns out, Charlotte's daughter never ended up, for some reason, going to Carnegie Drama School. So much for prearranged campus tours.

By April of 1962, Evelyn Rose and Ray's splitsville final,

FROM THE BACK OF THE HOUSE

Evelyn Rose (that moved out again) had moved out. Fact of the matter, all Ray's amours had to move out. Ray worked there, lived above the joint, come thick, thin, or raw he stayed put at 1800 Scranton Road.

It should be noted Cheri and her mother (passing time back in PA with Patricia's mother and father) visited Cleveland when I drove back in town from Michigan State for breaks, holiday, long weekends.

After the Rockey divorce II (whispers suggest the pay off to Evelyn Rose was much less than $100,000 and more than $10,000), Evelyn Rose moved to an apartment in Parma. With a new career path as hair stylist, she graduated from Grace College of Cosmetology and began work there as an instructor in shampoo, rinse, cut, color and set. It should also be noted after Evelyn Rose moved out, Cheri and her mother, when in Cleveland, bunked in with Evelyn Rose but spent much time visiting Papa Ray at *the* Steak House.

In short order, the Rockey II final divorce decree issued, Charlotte and "my boy" tied the knot. Rockey III in the books, Charlotte officially became a member of the JIM'S clan. Stepping onto *the* Steak House stage, the fate-weavers dizzy dizzy dizzy, the beginning of the Charlotte era (circa 1964) got officially entered into Ray Rockey's win-loss validation of the Cleveland Flat's world records.

35

ICING ON THE CAKE

Charlotte, firmly ensconced in the JIM'S family routine, now broke bread with across-the-hall neighbors–Aunt Hilda, Uncle Frank, and Aunt Mickey. Icing on the cake, she held the title (never mind number three) "daughter-in-law" to Aunt Hilda. What is it they say, three on a match? Depends on who's counting and whose book of matches.

Anyway, Charlotte's roots deepening daily in affairs' clan, shortly after her debut, the curtain went up on her entrance into Jim's Steak House business matters. One of her first suggestions had Ray taking Mondays off. A little background: Ray, in more than thirty years of tending "baby," seldom took an hour off let alone a day. Even the day JIM'S was closed (Sunday) he spent the mornings totaling up Saturday night's take and counting empty liquor bottles. The new Monday-off routine, Charlotte reasoned, allowed a two-day weekend (Sunday and Monday), they could do things (no yawning please) together.

Soon thereafter, Ray tending a little less of "baby," Charlotte got herself promoted to bean-counter in charge. Shorthand, she handled the dough–payables, receivables, and deposits.

It should be noted that Tony (remember him, the assistant manger) used to do payables and receivables but, well you know . . . he still got to manage the scullers and take

FROM THE BACK OF THE HOUSE

inventory.

In the meantime, Charlotte and Ray roamed a bit–Spain, Mexico, the Carribean. The old hand-me-down travel spots (Sarasota, Put-in-Bay) of Ray and Evelyn Rose were verboten by the new Mrs. Rockey. Not unusual, actually understandable.

Related to verboten, Ray sold his share in the Put-in-Bay cottage and bought (bets are 10 to 1 on whose idea) a mini farm with a nice house near Charlotte's hometown of Bristol, Virginia.

Long "do something together" regularly included (a couple hours drive south on I-77) Sunday-Monday "weekends" at the Tennessee ranch. Ray especially loved it. He bought a small tractor to mow grass, and cultivated a patch of dirt where he planted a vegetable garden. The vegetable garden proving a point–Ray was a planter at heart. Actually, every chance he got he planted–vegetables, flowers, trees, and whatnots.

For example, where 200 years ago Native Americans grew maize, he sowed corn next to *the* Steak House lawn. Not much to show for it (rats ate it), he enjoyed knowing something had been planted. One time, on JIM'S lawn next to the Cuyahoga river, he planted a few peach trees. Peaches ripening nicely, one morning going out to pick some fruit, he stood in shocked silence. All the peached gone, picked clean, some "&%$#" had ripped him off. Morose mixed with fury,

FROM THE BACK OF THE HOUSE

taking it personally, he considered it grand theft but who could he accuse let alone sue. He vowed to plant again.

But most of all he loved flowers. Thousands were planted around *the* Steak House lawn. In later years, the JIM'S "girls" doing the work, Raymond sipped a cool one in the shade while supervising the planting. True to his first love, later in the evening, supervision relinquished, he might do some planting of his own.

36

Accolades

In any case, things clicking, Ray and Charlotte in locked step tending "baby," the accolades for JIM'S came pouring in. Here's one from Cleveland Press writer, Bill Dvorak:

> STEAKS ARE SHIPSHAPE ON COLLISION BEND
> From the window tables in Jim's Steak House, at 1800 Scranton Rd. in the Flats, diners have an unobstructed backdoor view of the heart of Cleveland, including the Terminal group of buildings. This is impressive day or night, fair weather or foul.
> During the shipping season freighters inching around Collision Bend often beam their searchlights into the glass enclosed dining room by way of greeting, and even in the winter, with river traffic at a halt, there are lights and life aboard vessels tied up nearby along the Cuyahoga.
> Our colleague Winsor French . . . once enthused in print, "surely one of the most spectacular restaurants in the country," and bracketed this phrase with "breathtaking" and "dramatic." . . . Manager is Raymond Rockey
> (Bill Dvorak, The Cleveland Press, Jan 10, 1964)

The Dvorak story was accompanied by a photo of Ray standing in JIM'S main dining room with a menu in hand ready to host. The Press version is captioned in part, "In foreground is Raymond Rockey, restaurant manager . . ."

FROM THE BACK OF THE HOUSE

Original Press photo courtesy Cleveland State University Library

Holy Toledo! Picture and name in the newspaper, Ray basking in the glow like a just baked pretzel came another kind review from who else, none other than Winsor French:

> I can hardly believe it but Ray Rockey, after all these years as manager of Jim's Steak House, clinging to the shores of Collision Bend way down there in the flats, has finally seen the light and the potential of his own restaurant. Rockey, in fact, has ordered 12 umbrella tables, each seating four people, and any day now will be scattering them on the front lawn around the weeping willows. Tush, at long last, you will be able to sit out of doors over dinner or a drink, watching the river traffic glide by while the city's skyline provides a spectacular and dramatic backdrop, especially at night when it

FROM THE BACK OF THE HOUSE

looks like towering jeweled curtain. And if a speck of dust falls into your highball or onto your steak, for heaven's sake don't complain. Just pretend you are in Paris, Rome or Naples, three well-spoken-of cities that also are not free of dust. (Cleveland Press, circa 1965)

Umbrella tables on JIM'S lawn

Never mind the dust, Ray (Charlotte nudging) was on a roll. He continued to upgrade JIM'S by putting in docking space along the river and a wooden walkway. This is where The *Good Time* sight seeing boat wintered for many years. Again Mr. French took notice:

> . . .installed [at Jim's Steak House] is a new . . . gangplank . . . if you own a yacht or even a rowboat, it would be possible to steam up the river . . . anchor and have dinner.
> Also, when the Indians are playing night games

FROM THE BACK OF THE HOUSE

> in the Stadium JIM'S offers a package deal. You dine there, cruise down river on the Goodtime to Gate A, see the game, then cruise back . . . of course, there is no parking problem . . . (Winsor French, Cleveland Press, 1965)

In and around the flattering "ink," and Charlotte spit shines, things flowing merrily along, JIM'S (Ray by proxy) got Frenched yet again:

> One of nicest places in town to have lunch during these last summer days is on the lawn of Jim's Steak House at the river's edge. It is even more spectacular at dinner, of course, when the skyline becomes a glittering backdrop and the river with its bridges leaping out of the shadows assumes an aura of mystery . . . tables with their gay umbrellas are scattered at random under the weeping willows, there is almost always a breeze and if a freighter happens to be inching its way around Collision Bend you get quite a show along with your meal . . .
> (Cleveland Press, August 31, 1966 W. French)

And (heaven to Betsy) Frenched once more:

> IT'S A DELIGHT TO DINE BY RIVER
> Jim's Steak House has had those café tables with their huge umbrellas out on the lawn for some time now and dining there in the evening is a joy.
> You are right beside the river, with the city's

FROM THE BACK OF THE HOUSE

skyline serving as a backdrop. Now and then, a freighter drifts by. As dusk falls the river takes on a sheen, the debris becomes invisible, the water all lights and shadows.

Draw bridges rise and fall and it is all very romantic. This, in fact, could be Europe - the River Seine, the Danube or even the Tiber- not the polluted Cuyahoga.

Also, I am happy to report the management has remembered again how to cut properly thick steaks, and steaks are all they serve out of doors. Be warned though, it is on the expensive side. (Cleveland Press, Circa 1966)

Expensive side! The Seine, The Danube. The Tiber! . . . Winsor!

Amid the celebration came more praise from a certain Ms. Escargot, November 25, 1966 in the Plain Dealer:

STEAKS BY THE RIVER

It is not unusual for a stranger to come away from the High Level Bridge muttering something about a mirage . . . There it was down there in the middle of all those factories, warehouse and smokestacks.

An oasis of green grass, swaying palm trees and a bubbling spring. At this point, a native Clevelander lays a hand upon the poor soul's arm and explains that yes, indeed, he did spy a patch of greenery nestled in the brown, black and gray drabness of the Flats . . . it's not a mirage at all but Jim's Steak House, a picturesque restaurant that's been on the

FROM THE BACK OF THE HOUSE

banks of Collision Bend since 1931.

And again Ms. Escargot in the Plain Dealer, December 8, 1967:

> VIEW, FOOD UNBEATABLE AT JIM'S STEAK HOUSE
> . . . [JIM's] one of Cleveland's favorite dining places . . . sits on the river bank at the famed Collision Bend. It is set off by beautiful weeping willow and birch trees . . . The view . . . is worth the price of the evening alone . . . the lights from a thousand Terminal Tower windows dance on its waters, it's all romance and wonder . . . Manager Ray Rockey greets you at the door and sees to your every need . . . Some evening if you find yourself romantically inclined and hungry at the same time, may we suggest a trip to the Flats—Jim's Steak House can solve both your problems.

Wow! Maybe Ray bumped into Ms. Escargot at the bar or maybe she contacted him. Whatever, given her nice reviews (all the talk of romance and amour coupled with Raymond's propensity for planting) dollars to donuts "my boy" rubbed more than Escargot's something under a JIM's window-side table.

And just when it was time to eat some protein, enter another (sounds French to me) Frenchman, one Jacques G. LeGrand, writing in the Plain Dealer, October 10, 1969:

FROM THE BACK OF THE HOUSE

a steak house. I did and was pleasantly surprised with the quaintness and quality of the establishment, a place called Jim's Steak House, 1800 Scranton Road.

JIM'S squats on the banks of the Cuyahoga River at a location known as collision Bend. It is a veritable oasis of greenery amidst the brick buildings and steel bridges of the Flats area . . . lovely willows and clumps of birches grace the river front and lend an air of freshness to the scene. The view is especially enchanting when the darkness of evening hides the defects of the sullied river and the lights from a thousand office windows reflect on the water. One need not be French to feel the romance of it all.

. . . JIM'S is a steakhouse, nothing more, nor less . . . the restaurant has between five and seven tons of it [steak] on hand at all times. Nothing but prime beef is served. It is light of bark and nicely marbled to insure the utmost in tenderness. Any cut imaginable is yours for the ordering and prices are in line with the city's better restaurants. Sirloin strips range from $6.50 to $8.25, T-Bones from $4.60 to $7.50, while filet mignon runs from $5 to $7. . . . The strip steak I ordered was perfectly attuned to my taste, crispy outside, pink and juicy inside. Let me recommend the house' hash-browned potatoes and the French-fried onion rings. Both are served in generous portions. The lettuce salad was crackling fresh. The service is quite good . . . the only complaint I had . . . The mushrooms left something to be desired and there was a lack of good hard rolls.

Lack of good hard rolls! Any doubt the guy was French?

FROM THE BACK OF THE HOUSE

Whatever, after the LaGrande ink, hundred to one, Ray and company nursed celebration hangovers for a month of Sundays.

And so it went "down there in the Flats," JIM'S basking in success (according to Ray, grossing a million-two plus or minus a year), Raymond savoring the "ink," bean counter Charlotte, supervising the gazintas and gazoutas, whispered in Raymond's ear that a better way to "gazintas" might exist.

It went like this: Ray and Charlotte founded a food brokerage firm from which Jim's Steak House, Inc. (that would be Aunt Hilda) bought sundry and assorted food stuffs. Tack on 15%, a wink, smile (don't tell Hilda), and thank you very much. Some call it cooking something. Others say, in the best tradition of humanity's march to more, "Business is business." What's wrong with that. Look around.

Anyway, while "my boy" basked in rave reviews, tulips, panties, and knickers; Charlotte (JIM'S bean counter in charge) double clutched the brokerage firm. Above all she kept score. Whatever else the Lady from Bristol was, beneath the la belle smile, she possessed a bottom line, pit bull doggedness that got the bone every time and then some.

37
WAIT IN LINE

Skipping back, following Ray and Evelyn Rose's divorce, Evelyn Rose, after a few years teaching beautician students at Grace College, opened in Seven Hills, *Evelyn Rockey Creative Coiffures*. Late 60's, haute coiffure in vogue, six beauticians hauteing, Evelyn Rose: "Color job around fifty buck, we raked it in hand over fist . . . all in all did pretty

Street sign, top left/center, EVELYN

good."

What's this got to do with Jim's Steak House? In over-the-back-yard fence chatter, it's "doing pretty good" that keeps

FROM THE BACK OF THE HOUSE

life's mysteries interesting. Namely, "My boy" getting word of that "doing pretty good" line, soon thereafter began making regular visit (incognito of course, Charlotte was busy with gazinta) to the beauty shop.

Hello.

As the shop proprietor (that would be Evelyn Rose) put it, "Hell, he was out here every week. Got a haircut, manicure."

The proprietor continued, "Then he stopped coming, got mad at Marissa." (Marissa did manicures.)

"Why?"

"She made him wait in line. How many times did he make people wait in line at *the* Steak House?"

Ray may have quit waiting for haircuts but, like that penny, he kept coming back, sending letters (money included), kept in touch, maintained ties, he even sent meat Evelyn Rose's way.

We'll never know Ray's reasons or motives, torn between some whatever, for his "coming back," but a short side trip might shed some light:

Remember yours truly, pursuing that sheep skin at Michigan State, 1961-63. Well, after Evelyn Rose left *the* Steak House, moved to Parma, Cheri and her mother, Patricia (when not in Pennsylvania), stayed with Evelyn Rose. Yours truly back and forth to Parma, in addition to Cheri, were conceived and born three additional offsprings–fraternal

FROM THE BACK OF THE HOUSE

twin's Ray and Tami, and Karen. The four children became affectionately known to Ray and Evelyn Rose as "the kids."*

"THE KIDS" – Ray, Tami, Karen, Cheri

Amidst the quagmire of Freudian delight, back to "he even sent meat Evelyn Rose's way." Seems Ray had delivered (from various JIM'S meat suppliers) on a regular basis, freezer loads of choice cuts to Evelyn Rose's house (beauty business "doing pretty good" she had bought a three-bedroom brick ranch on Day Drive) in Parma. One story goes, Ray directing, a meat packer's delivery truck backed up to Evelyn Rose's back door, filled her freezer with "steaks, roasts, chops, you name it."

As to Ray "sending letters (money included," here's one of several, handwritten by him circa 1966 (Jim's letterhead and sent in a JIM'S envelope) to Evelyn Rose:

FROM THE BACK OF THE HOUSE

That "kind of" P.S. at the end 'for you and the kid's' meant

FROM THE BACK OF THE HOUSE

cash.

Evelyn Rose: "Usually two, three hundred dollars. Whatever else, he had a good heart. If a [JIM'S] waitress overcharged a customer for something, Ray going over receipts next day, finding the mistake, he'd call the customer, make it right."

While you're figuring it all out, some more marital intrigue adding angst to the grist:

Recall Ray taking Monday's off so he and Charlotte could do things together. Well, it seems a lady customer of Evelyn Rose's beauty shop had tickets to an upcoming Playhouse Square production of *Hello Dolly*. The play a couple weeks away, friend invited Evelyn Rose to join her and a couple other ladies to go see the hot musical. Tickets were for a Monday night.

Light bulbs flashing in Evelyn Rose's mind (no secrets front, back, past, or present in the JIM'S inner house circle, she had spies inside JIM'S), knowing Monday was Ray's night off, she suggested dinner at Jim's Steak House before the show.

So, responding to the lady with the tickets to *Hello Dolly*, probably a mischievous smile on her face, Evelyn Rose said, "Sounds good."

Waiting until the Monday before the *Hello Dolly* ladies night out, knowing it was Ray's day off, Evelyn Rose called,

FROM THE BACK OF THE HOUSE

made reservation, "Dinner for four, next Monday, E. Rockey."

Confirmed by the results you are about to learn, sometime after Evelyn Rose booked the dinner, Ray (Evelyn Rose knew he would, he scanned it hourly) checked the reservation book. Yep, there it was–*E. Rockey-4, Monday, 6:30 p.m.*.

Bingo. Guess who's coming to dinner?

6:30 p.m. Monday (Ray's day off) when in strolled the Parma theater group, surprise. Ray stood at JIM'S host stand. Cheese cake smile, he greeted the entourage, seated them at a nice window table, spieled off the specials of day, wrapping it up with, "And the Steaks better be good."

Evelyn Rose and ladies: "I'm sure, thank you, goody goody."

An hour or so later, as they left, Evelyn Rose recounts the scene: "When we were leaving, walked past the table at the entrance where Ray always sat, he stood like a little trooper. Charlotte had joined him. She didn't stand, didn't smile, actually looked like she had bitten an olive pit. Tony Liotta, (the assistant manger, remember) seated there too, didn't know whether to stand or go blind. Poor guy."

In any case, a few days after the incident, a typed letter to Evelyn Rose arrived from Charlotte:

"Your presence at the steak house at any time is neither wanted nor appreciated. Speaking for myself, my husband, and Mrs. Mercurio, no one here has any desire to see you or

FROM THE BACK OF THE HOUSE

hear from you . . ."

    Well shucks, read it for yourself:

> Your presence at the steak house at any time is neither wanted nor appreciated. Speaking for myself, my husband, and Mrs. Mercurio, no one here has any desire to see you or hear from you for any reason whatsoever. It is my personal opinion that you show very bad taste, as well as an enormous lack of pride and self-respect. To avoid an awkward situation for all concerned, and possible great embarassment to you, kindly avail yourself of other public places in the future.
>
> I trust I have made myself clear, and that no further word on the subject will be necessary.
>
> *Charlotte Rockey*

FROM THE BACK OF THE HOUSE

OUCH!

Seeming to indicate something sinister was afoot in the Ray and Charlotte marital bed of roses, the "ouch" letter reported to Raymond by Evelyn Rose, he wrote back:

5-21-67

Dear Evie

Sorry I didn't get back to you yesterday but I know nothing of what you mentioned anyhow. I will talk to you Wed. I have done nothing for the kids of late so take and get them something for Seomada —

I'm sorry for what ever happened —

As usual, "I have done nothing for the kids of late" equaled

FROM THE BACK OF THE HOUSE

$$$ enclosed. Further letters from Ray to Evelyn Rose indicate the bloom (who knows what goes on *Between Sheets* and *Angel's Tit)* was coming off the Charlotte shine much earlier. Witness this letter:

JIM'S STEAK HOUSE 1800 SCRANTON ROAD. CLEVELAND 13, OHIO CH 1-4454

Buy the kids, Patty & yourself something for Easter — This should be enough. Don't say where they came from and don't mention it to noone & burn this note. What people don't know don't hurt them.

Hmmm, (Evelyn Rose, for whatever reason, obviously

FROM THE BACK OF THE HOUSE

didn't burn the note), "what people don't know don't hurt them . . ." Wonder who that referred to?

Be that as it may, adding further to the marital intrigue, there stewed in the JIM'S bigger kettle of fish, a new romance evolving. Goes like this: You remember Tony Liotta. Traipsing the JIM'S stage like a butler in a three-act play, he and Ray graduated Benedictine together, best man at Evelyn and Ray's marriage, now getting the greased shaft from daughter-in-law number three, A.K.A., Mrs. Charlotte Rockey. **

Turns out during all those good and plenty years at JIM'S, Tony and Evelyn Rose became pals. So T, as Tony was known, being an eyewitness to the *Hello Dolly* incident at JIM'S front door, privy to the poison pen letter from Charlotte, and the stuff that hit the fan later, called Evelyn Rose.

We can't know for sure, but imagine it went something like this:

"Hi Eve (he called her Eve) you shoulda heard what happened after you guys left . . . it really hit the fan . . . I know . . . she is that . . . have tickets to a show . . ."

So, whatever adult altar boys do on dates, Tony and Evelyn Rose clicked, dated and . . . woops.

Recall, no secrets front or back, past or present in the inner JIM'S house circle. Ditto Cleveland's restaurant community. Cooks, waitresses, bartenders going back sixteen generations are like a family of flies. Naturally, the grapevine

FROM THE BACK OF THE HOUSE

humming, Charlotte got the skinny about T and Evelyn Rose dating.

Never mind Charlotte shoving "my boy" up the stairs to Tootsie's kitchen, just imagine the scene when Ray, Charlotte at his side, broke the news to Aunt Hilda about Tony's new steady. No doubt about it, Hilda known to sling things, more than #$# hit the kitchen walls, and for sure Uncle Frank didn't get fresh raspberries that night.

A little later, Ray to Tony:

"Hey T, I heard you are engaged to Evelyn."

Yep. "Can't work here."

"But peeoc." (Pronounced P-ock, that's what Tony called Ray, don't ask me what it means, it's Italian for something, maybe some paesano derivative, if it's nasty send me a note.)

Ray: "No, nope, Tootsie threw a kitchen knife."

"Okay."

And that was that, except (about a year later) an excuse-a-mia: Tony and Evelyn Rose's trip down the aisle a few days around the corner, Evelyn got cold feet, backed out and that is yet another story. Short of it, Tony got blued, tattooed, and that other thing too. *

Longtime bartender Angelo Rich was made assistant manager. Angelo Rich, slick, fast, matinee idol, Italian's Italian. Thin not from lack of food, that other thin, too much of it. Suffice it to say, for a time he lived on a forty-foot something Chris Craft cabin cruiser that he docked at East

FROM THE BACK OF THE HOUSE

55th Street Marina. Boating down the Cuyahoga to JIM'S and his assistant management duties, he more than not got delayed by Cleveland weather, dodging river traffic, lady boaters, and/or waiting for a lift bridge or two or three. This exasperated Ray and Angelo's "Can't help it boss, have to wait for bridges to go up," didn't help the matter any. Angelo's assistant manager duties lasted a while then he was gone.

---

* Ray bought each of the kids a car when they graduated from high school, paid their college tuition, had trusts set up for their kid's college fund, and much more. He could have cut it all loose with a word but he never did. A wrenching sad note, Karen, in 2003 (just 38), lost a battle with breast cancer. Survived by her husband Matt and Nicholas, Morgan, and Madison.

**Tony later went into business with John Pistoni and managed the Lincoln Inn near Public Square.

38

BEGINNING OF THE END

What is it somebody said, all good things must come to an end, something like that, but why is it that way? Why isn't it written all bad things must come to an end? Looked it up, goes back to about 1374 A.D., Chaucer* - "There is an end to everything." Makes sense, "There is an end to everything." You can buy that. Doesn't take a brain surgeon, look around, everything ends. But when the Chaucer's words hit, around 1600 A.D., the U. S. of A., some half baked word sausage maker, with little nuances that could drive a State Fair judge wacky, fed it into his word grinder and out came, "All *good* things must come to an end."

That's why it's said that way. It's from the slippery hands of a maker of word sausage. And so a way of sick thinking is burned into a culture psyche, religion, upbringing, whatever. The curse of the half empty glass thing that infects early and eats away until the maggots arrive. It's the fear of losing something you had nothing to do with but forever think you did. It's the fear of not pleasing and forever atoning, trying to fill a half empty glass that has a bastard hole in the bottom.

Past the huffing sermonizing, at Jim's Steak House "end things" stuffed in the grinder past poignant, turns out the "good" word sausage maker got one thing right when, in 1963, a "good" came to an end.

With a healthy dose of reality and a little poetic license, it

229

goes like this: Not one to forget, Charlotte (after the whole mess with Tony and Evelyn Rose, not to mention that kowtowing to Evelyn Rose and her *Hello Dolly* theater group) ambled daily over to Hilda's side of the penthouse for morning coffee and a chat. Settling at the kitchen table, over whole wheat toast and black coffee, many things got sausaged into Hilda's ear.

Top among things: Evelyn Rose, the nerve, and that Tony (Charlotte couldn't say dago, wop, or guinea, Frank might hear) back stabber. Second cup of coffee warmed up, things got closer to the bone when Charlotte hinted there lived and breathed an enemy in the camp.

Hilda: "Who?"

Pause while Charlotte darts a nod back the hall to Aunt Mickey's bedroom.

"No."

"Yes."

The meaning was clear: Ethel May McCue, A. K. A, Aunt Mickey, Raymond's Dolly, was the enemy.

Charlotte: "She and that Evelyn Rose thing are like sisters, always have been, they meet secretly for lunch, have been since that (expletive deleted, begins with f) bitch left."

Third cup, Charlotte could hardly contain herself. "The Irish bitch (that would be Mickey) is a sister spy in the closet to that other bitch, Evelyn."

FROM THE BACK OF THE HOUSE

In a nut shell, Charlotte was legal, Mrs. Raymond Rockey (forget about third), daughter-in-law (ditto third) and "Damn it, law is law. McCue is a %$#$ guest, paid help."

What other sharp, flats, and whole notes Charlotte minced, diced, and tinned into Aunt Hilda's ear we'll never know but don't forget, Charlotte always got the bone.

Evelyn, Ray, Aunt Mickey in happier times

Piece by piece into the great human word grinder, the crushing full bore, Aunt Mickey woke up every morning to a word dropped here, a cutting remark there, a whisper overheard everywhere and, the "sausage" unending, a heart can only take so much.

And thus the inevitable, June 1963, just five months before Jack Kennedy flew to Dallas, the world in some kind of nutty change mood, Ray's Dolly, 63 years in the "word meat market," in the best Tennyson rhyme or reason tradition, "crossed the bar."**

---

*Random House Dictionary of Popular Proverbs and Sayings, Gregory Y. Titelman, Random House, New York, 1996

**To many Aunt Mickey didn't really die, she just returned home to be with her winged friends

39
CRACK IN THE DAM

Not long after Aunt Mickey crossed the bar, "ends" inching along like a crack in a dam, Uncle Frank pulled into a gas station on St. Clair to fill up. Refueling complete (they had attendants then) a Jim's Steak House credit card receipt presented for signing, Frank didn't know who he was let alone what he had for lunch. The gas station attendant called *the* Steak House and Ray beat a hasty rescue. Long and short, Alzheimer had claimed the man of a thousand smiles and a million raspberry sundaes.

Frank (pinky ring on right hand pinky) in happier times

Aunt Hilda's attempt to keep Frank at home failed. "All hours, day and night, he just ran away." One time Ray caught him heading up Eagle Ramp dressed only in his white Jockey boxer shorts.

The choice coming down to none or less, life's muck resurfacing for Hilda, she placed Frank in a nursing home.

FROM THE BACK OF THE HOUSE

Ray's Dolly gone, Uncle Frank in a nursing home, marital "bliss" on the Rockey side of the penthouse was like Aunt Hilda's wind damaged willow tree–steel cables strained to keep it from toppling.

Alas, one "validation" by "my boy" too many, (it's rumored both Ray and Charlotte were setting new records) the cables snapped and Charlotte split to the farm in Bristol.

An email (names blanked to protect the innocent) from on-the-scene daughter Cheri sums up "my boys" validating activity:

From: <crourke--@____>
To: <--rockey@____>
Subject: Re: JIM'S/dad/pa pa
Date: Tuesday, October 25, 2005 9:32 PM

I'm not sure what caused Charlotte to leave. It may have been [Blank #1's] sister. She was the really young one. [Blank #1's sister] was in and out of the picture, mostly when she needed money. [Blank #2] came along in the mid '80's. She was the nut case who had the house in Mexico. She was only around for a while then she was more or less on the fringe. There was also that [Blank #3] who I think he [Ray] actually wanted to marry. Like I said, it was pretty crazy at times.

In the meantime, middle, and before the "fat lady sang," suggesting somehow a meaning in it all, the former relationship between Hilda and daughter-in-law II, Evelyn Rose, began to glow anew. The renewed bonding began when, out of the blue, a honcho at Frank's nursing home called to inform Ray, "There's some blond babe keeps coming

FROM THE BACK OF THE HOUSE

to visit Frank, just thought you'd like to know."

Ray mentioned it to Hilda.

Her immediate reply, "Gotta be Evelyn."

And it was.

Aunt Hilda not in excellent health, she and Evelyn Rose's bond never really severed, they often visited Frank at the home. Evelyn Rose: "Frank, a proud man, you know we would visit him and, for brief glimpses, you know, especially in the morning, he would remember, say, 'Don't let anybody know I'm in this place.'"

40

THE DAM BREAKS

Raymond and Charlotte splitsvilled (technically not divorced, she lived on the farm in Bristol, Ray lived where he always lived, above JIM's) Ray remained Aunt Hilda's Huckleberry Finn, Tom Sawyer, "my boy."

For instance, in a chapter out of Hilda's "my boy" book there occurred a sort of Ray and Evelyn Rose mini-reconciliation holiday gathering. Hilda, Ray, Evelyn Rose, "the kids," their mother Patricia, yours truly assembled in the JIM'S penthouse for drinks and dinner. Shortly before dinner dessert, a telephone call came for Raymond. The call from Charlotte at Hopkins Airport (remember she had relocated to Bristol) she needed a lift to a friend's house. Ray, looking like a heel on a worn penny loafer, put his coat on and left to pick her up. You could see the pain in Aunt Hilda's eyes. But what's a "my boy" stepmother to do. Some awkward sighs, hems, haws, nothing more said, Evelyn Rose put Hilda to bed and gathered guests melted away back to Parma.

Thinking about it, one wonders what hold Charlotte had on Ray. A taxidermy take on it might be that Ray, a sentimental guy, would rather have stuffed his "trophies" and hung them on a wall. Absent that (Freudian psycho babble and Les Roberts' validation theory aside), who knows what dogged him.

Anyway, life for Aunt Hilda (first husband's untimely

FROM THE BACK OF THE HOUSE

death, diabetic, heart failing, eyesight dimmed by cataracts, "my boy" at it again, "other boy" in a nursing home–in) the words of Hemingway, "bitched from the beginning," the crack widened beyond wide and the dam broke.

The Plain Dealer obit:

> Mrs. Mercurio dies; was Flats restaurateur. Mrs. Frank Mercurio, 75, better known as Mrs. Jim, cofounder, owner and president of Jim's Steak House, 1800 Scranton Rd., SW, died yesterday in Grace Hospital. Her home was at the business address. Mrs. Mercurio, the former Hilda T. Hoffman, born in Pittsburgh, came here in 1920. She helped established the business, one of the best known Cleveland restaurants in the Flats, in 1929. The restaurant is at a point in the Cuyahoga River known as collision bend. Survivors besides her husband include two sons, [kind of] Raymond and Frank Jr.. Raymond now operates the business and is secretary-treasurer of the corporation.
> Services will be at St. Michael's Catholic Church, 3114 Scranton Rd. SW, at 10:00 a.m. Monday. (Plain Dealer, August 2, 1974)

Hilda laid out at Ripepi's, Frank still in the nursing home, there was some talk about bringing him to see her. That quickly got nixed with, "Hell, Frank don't know late from yesterday."

Mass for Hilda at St. Michael's on Scranton Road, the

FROM THE BACK OF THE HOUSE

white limo led procession (remember that crypt Frank bought umpteen years ago at Knollwood Mausoleum) proceeded to S.O.M. Center Road where Hilda was laid to rest in the bottom of four grotto slots.

With Hilda gone and Frank in a nursing home, Ray inherited a mother lode (some said elephant pile) of goodies and (after some token gifts to nephews and nieces) plenty of goodies landed in "my boys" lap. Some estimates put it in the six zero plus range with a two in front of the six zeros. Figure it out: three bedroom waterfront home (throw in a boat and dock) on Siesta Key, Florida; fifty or so acres (Uncle Frank had bought the plot back in the 50s) of undeveloped land five minutes from downtown Sarasota; cranking a million plus a year, Jim's Steak House, Inc.; plush six bedroom furnished penthouse above JIM'S. Tack on life insurance payout and the exact weight of the lode only the lawyers know for sure.

Not unexpected, Ray rolling in lode, getting-the-last-bone Charlotte high tailed it back from Bristol to 1800 Scranton Road where she, with a kiss on the cheek offered condolences to Ray. And, right out of a dime paperback, the estranged couple (vowing to take another stab at tip-toeing through the tulips) moved into the penthouse side of the living arrangements above JIM'S, and Uncle Frank and Aunt Hilda's bed.

Not far into the move, Frank, nine months after Hilda's death (perhaps sensing someone was sleeping in his bed) May

FROM THE BACK OF THE HOUSE

18, 1975, packed it in.

The Plain Dealer again:

> Frank P. Mercurio
> Funeral Mass was offered May 21 in St. Michael Church, Scranton Rd., for Frank P. Mercurio, 78, founder and owner of the old Standard Excavating Co. He died May 18 in the Aristocrat Nursing Home, Parma Hts.
> Mr. Mercurio headed Standard Excavating from the early 1940's until 1965, then helped his late wife operate Jim's Steak House in the Flats . . . (The Plain Dealer, May 1975)

Ripepi becoming one of the JIM'S family, services for Frank at St. Michael's, another limo led procession proceeded to S.O.M. Center Road.

Of the four slots in the grotto, the bottom occupied by Aunt Hilda, Franks was slipped into the one just above her. The grotto slot layering now looked like this:

> I-unoccupied
> II-unoccupied
> III-Uncle Frank
> IV-Aunt Hilda

Meantime back at JIM'S, the effort to sandblast away whole chapters of their paperback marriage coming up short, Charlotte split back to Bristol for good. The Charlotte JIM'S

FROM THE BACK OF THE HOUSE

era chiseled in stone, uptown lawyers hammered out a final who gets what, how much, and when.

On the spot Cheri's email take:

From: <crourke--@_____>
To: <--rockey@_____>
Subject: Re: JIM'S/dad/pa pa
Date: Tuesday, October 25, 2005 9:32 PM

...Charlotte still came into town a couple times a year and stayed at the Steak House while she went to doctor and dentist appointments. He [Ray] also periodically went to Virginia [Bristol] but this was less and less over time, probably not at all by the mid '80s. Charlotte was diagnosed with breast cancer and I think that is when he stopped going. She remained on the Steak House insurance for a long time, maybe up until his death. I'm not sure. He [Ray] also dated that older (compared to his usual choices) woman named [Blank #?]. He was a character in that respect.

PART IV
FALSE SPRING/INDIAN SUMMER

41

FALSE SPRING

In the late 1970's, almost like Cleveland mourned the loss of her "Queen of the Flats," the city had begun a slide down the famous slippery slope. Rust creeping though the Great Lake States like mold in a New Orleans pantry, the bottom fell out with Cleveland the first city to default since the Great Depression. Decline, decay, aging plants, lousy PR, blab from talk show host and media pundits had Cleveland branded, "The Mistake on the Lake."

It comes as no surprise, bottom of Eagle Ramp, 1800 Scranton Road, Ray Rockey (dry dipped in Vodka, taking care of anything that walked, crawled, or kneeled) woke up one morning to find Cleveland's downward pinch wasn't yesterday's hung over lady in pink. Matter of fact, keeping JIM'S open had become a drain on "my boy's" assets. Depleting bank account, all that inherited dough falling through more "cracks" than Squibb has pills, Ray resembled an actor having trouble with his lines.

Then, like it always does, or to date like it always does, when it seemed all of the castaways on Gillian's Island would never get rescued, a comeback. In short, Cleveland movers and shakers got their heads out of their pockets, broke out the check book and kick-started development with investments in steel, automobile, and other manufacturing.

Suddenly Cleveland trumpeted itself, The New America

FROM THE BACK OF THE HOUSE

City and, of particular note to this story, The Flat's Oxbow Association, founded in 1976, went to work promoting growth in, where else, the Flats. Suddenly, Cleveland's "smelly foot," once predominately (except for JIM'S) a manufacturing area, became a hotspot for dining and entertainment.

Once again coming out of that proverbial smelling like a rose, in 1979 Ray accepted CLEVELAND magazine's *Best Restaurant Award*.

Award in hand, scouring around for new ways to compete with the other just arrived Flats' joints, out of the blue up popped his granddaughter (remember his other "baby") Cheri.

A freshman at Texas A&M, visiting Cleveland for summer break, Cheri puts it this way: "I came to Ohio for the summer (or so I thought) in June of 1980. After a casual mention that I might be interested in the restaurant business. Next thing you know, I am on my way to visit the Culinary Institute in Hyde Park."

In short, Ray Rockey envisioned a new spring for JIM'S and (you have to assume) himself.

So, Cheri's just visiting turned to sign-up, she got accepted

FROM THE BACK OF THE HOUSE

at the Culinary Institute of America (CIA), Hyde Park, New York. Little catch: the Institute full up until July of '81, Texas A&M moot, she withdrew, moved to Cleveland, and began, while waiting for her (roughly a year later) CIA start date, interning at *the* Steak House.

Everything copasetic, things looking up, along came some press "ink" mixed with undertones of what would later flush out as a problem. The "ink" from The Journal Lorain, Ohio, Friday, August 29, 1980:

DINING OUT
JIM'S STEAK HOUSE GOOD AS EVER
BY LINDA GORDON

It's amazing: some 20 odd years have passed since my last visit to Jim's Steak House, and yet it's exactly as I remembered it - from the river view vista to the hot and crispy hash browns, it seems as if nothing has changed. Here is one place that has really stood the test of time.

The decor, which truth be known was considered almost painfully plain in its day, had - by not changing - taken on an air of originality. Starched white table linens, blond wood paneling, and a menu design [except the prices] that hasn't been altered since the early sixties give it something of the character of a period piece. And it appealed to us for its lack of pretense and its steadfast refusal to copycat whatever has been trendy at the moment . . .

FROM THE BACK OF THE HOUSE

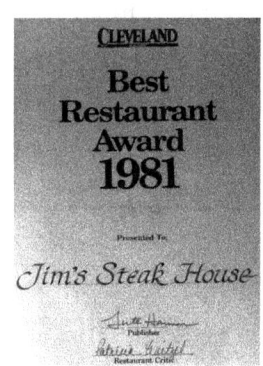

"Steadfast refusal to copycat" indeed. The undertone point: Ray prided tradition up to the end even when tradition was kicking him in the cha-ching. More on that later. But for now and nevertheless, his tradition pride paying off in the short term, after receiving CLEVELAND magazine's *Best Restaurant Award* in 1979, new "Cheri" hope in the air, JIM'S again got the Best award in 1980 and '81.

Then in 1982 came the same magazine's popular PEOPLE'S CHOICE AWARD.

Beyond local praise, the Steak House (also in 1982) received *The Stanley Blacker Fashion Award*. Least the Blacker award be dismissed, Brennan's of New Orleans and The Blue Fox of San Francisco were some other notables restaurants singled out by Blacker.

FROM THE BACK OF THE HOUSE

The Blacker award reads:
In recognition of your select cuisine; high standards of congenial service; inviting decor and ambience . . . and for your acknowledged reputation as one of the most favored and pleasurable dining establishments.

So much for awards, recognition, and shoot-the-moon spring promise.

42

Indian Summer

As planned, Cheri started classes at the CIA in July of `81, graduating a full-fledged chef in July`83. The press caught up a year later with the facts embellished (we assume) by proud "Papa":

> CHANGE OF PLANS, December 24, 1984 Plain Dealer
> Bill Hickey
> Ray Rockey, the proprietor of JIM'S Steak House, was considering an offer for his eatery on the Cuyahoga River's picturesque Collision Bend not long ago, but something happened that changed his mind.
> That something was his granddaughter, Cheri Rockey, 24, who moved here last month after working in restaurants in the East the past two years. She already has begun helping run JIM'S, long one of Cleveland's favorite dining places.
> No mere apprentice is the young woman from San Antonio, but a knowledgeable kitchen artist who graduated from the American Culinary Institute of Hyde Park, NY, after studying food and its preparation at Texas A&M.
> Ray Rockey, who was eight when his parents founded Jim's in 1930 and has worked there since his early teens, is pleased that the establishment will stay in the family. "When you've worked a lifetime to make something special, you're reluctant to turn it over to just anybody, no matter how much cash is

FROM THE BACK OF THE HOUSE

involved," he said. "When Cheri decided to come here, I couldn't have been more delighted."
Over the past 54 years Clevelanders have come to know Jim's Steak House as one of the most comfortable eating places in town. That is due largely to the family spirit Rockey infused in both the help, most of whom have been with him for years, and patrons.

Speaking of patrons, along into the second act, enter JIM'S stage left a middle age diva with black hair, heavy mascara, and a villa in Puerto Vallarta. A pitch woman with a flare, a knack, and a hank a hair, turns out she cast a hold on "my boy" in more ways than one.

She's the one Cheri mentioned back a-ways in an email: "[Blank] came along in the mid '80's . . . the nut case who had the house in Mexico."

Turns out, the "nut case" whispering in Raymond's whatever, coupled with a desire to debunk his steadfast refusal to change image (not to mention business slipping further south), he began an Art Deco make-over of Jim's Steak House. A few months later, his bank account two notches below sucked dry, the job finished, the joint's interior looked like Paul Gauguin had come back from the dead and, let loose in the wine cellar, had attacked the wine maker.

Arriving patrons were treated to a wall mural (dripping in deep reds, pale greens, palm trees and naked natives) eight feet long and three feet high hanging in the vestibule. New red and black carpeting covered the floors, and surreal paintings on the cocktail lounge walls gave new meaning to phallic symbols.

Ray and guests in front of new mural

Symbols, sugar plum fairies, something, dancing in his imagination, Ray went for broke. He had the JIM'S kitchen remodeled with state of the art dish washer, gas stoves, coolers, the works. Not only that, other places in the flats (people liked to party, drink, dine outside), seemed they all had a deck. So Ray put in a deck, seated around fifty. The waitress hated it. "Have to work out there in the heat

Deck under red awning

FROM THE BACK OF THE HOUSE

with the bugs and sweat and (expletive deleted) ugh." Even Ray lamented, "Rains every weekend from May to September." Nevertheless, to extend the deck's use into late Fall, he had space heaters installed to lengthen the deck experience into early Spring and late Fall.

Other things were upgraded, added, walkways, so many flower gardens the outside environs looked like a regular botanical garden

At one time in here, Ray considered encasing the roof over the main dining room in glass, making a lounge, had the blue prints drawn up, was going to call the joint RAYMOND'S APARTMENT, elevator and all, but the cost (financial things were further south than south) was too much.

Ray like that one legged man in a butt kicking contest, entering stage left and right, were diva pitch women with a flare, a knack, and a hank a hair who held sway on Ray in more ways than one.

43

Go For It

Decks, space heaters, bugs, rain, two years later, spinning the Cheri angle for yet another drop of go-for-it, a story in Northeast Ohio Business & Industry, January 1985 . . . read it for yourself:

NORTHEAST OHIO BUSINESS & INDUSTRY
Venerable steak house welcomes new generation
Jan. 1985

You know a restaurant is more than a restaurant when a sign goes up on a main street, directing traffic to it.

On January 8, a sign with the words "Jim's Steak House" and an arrow will be erected on E. 9th Street, at the top of the Eagle Street descent into Cleveland's flats. At the foot of that hill, just across the drawbridge, is a dining institution that has been a favorite of Cleveland area business people and families for more than 50 years.

Founded by Jim Rockey in 1930, Jim's is now run by his son, Ray, with Ray's granddaughter, Cheri, now taking a more and more active role in management.

"We've stayed good by staying the same over the years," notes Rockey.

Featuring carefully aged USDA Prime steaks, fresh seafoods and other delights (including Rocky Mountain trout flown in from Denver three days each week), Jim's is as well known for its location — a little over an arm's reach from huge ore boats wending their way through the sharp bends of the Cuyahoga River.

"The one thing that has changed is our customer mix," says Rockey. "There's a whole new and younger generation that's discovering us, and that's great."

Part of the reason for that shift is the involvement of his daughter, Cheri Lynn, a graduate of the Culinary Institute at Hyde Park, N.Y.

"Just as I relate with the long time customers from the steel and shipping industries, she relates with the younger crowd that's moving up."

Now in his 60's, Rockey can't remember a day when he wasn't helping out at Jim's. "It's like taking care of a baby that never grows up."

Reservations are strongly recommended. Call 241-6343. Private rooms are available.

Cheri Lynn Rockey at the helm at Jim's.

255

And then there was this in TRAVEL HOST, circa 1986:

Jim's Steak House on the Cuyahoga River at Collision Bend, has the mark of a successful restaurant, longevity (celebrating 56 years).

A favorite dining spot for Clevelanders over the years, its landmark reputation brings people from far distant places.

Cheri and guest

Today, Cleveland's oldest steak house in continuous operation by the same family since 1930, also features fresh seafood.

Ray Rockey, owner/manager, personally greets guests arriving for lunch or dinner. Rockey takes great pride in not only the quality of food served, but also in the grounds surrounding the restaurant. Spring finds thousands of tulips, crocus and daffodils, along with flowering shrubs in full bloom.

The main dining room has three glass window walls, affording an excellent view of the garden's changing scene, Cleveland's Terminal Tower and the Cuyahoga River . . . Diners who rate restaurants not only on food (excellent) and food service (waitresses are outstanding), but on appointments as well, will appreciate the

FROM THE BACK OF THE HOUSE

> sparkling white linen tablecloths, napkins and attractive place settings which remind one of blue sails.
> Boaters enjoy the docking privileges provided diners at Jim's . . .
> Open daily for luncheon, 11:00 a.m. to 4:00 p.m. Jim's serves dinner beginning at 4:00 p.m.. Monday through Saturday (closed Sundays and holidays. For window table reservations call 241-6343. Separate bar, private dining room can accommodate 10-60. All major credit cards accepted.

Alas, reality (newspaper or no) being what it is, here is the definitive skinny on the resuscitation effort at JIM'S from the CIA graduate, prima chef, Cheri Lynn (Rockey) Rourke:

From: <crourke--@__
To: <--rockey@__
Subject: Re: JIM'S/dad/pa pa
Date: Sunday, October 23, 2005 9:39 PM
Hi Dad

... the 80's were not a particularly wonderful decade for me . . . I came to Ohio for the summer (or so I thought) in June of 1980. Next thing I know after a casual mention that I might be interested in the restaurant business, I am on my way to visit the Culinary Institute in Hyde Park. Nice place but I think I'd rather finish my Bachelor's Degree and then decide. No can do says PaPa and the next thing I know I'm driving to Hyde Park in July of 1981 after doing another year towards my Bachelor's degree at Baldwin Wallace while working Full time at the restaurant. I graduated from the CIA in March of 1983 and went to work for Service Systems, Inc as the kitchen magager at Blossom Music Center. "To get experience" says Papa even though that wasn't part of the original deal when I was sent to Hyde Park.

FROM THE BACK OF THE HOUSE

Honestly, I think that things were already starting to fall off financially and he was having second thoughts about bringing me on board. Anyway, after Blossom I continued to work for Service Systems at Allstate Insurance in Hudson managing their cafeteria. I hated it. I was making less than 20,000 a year and trying to pay for an apartment and a car. I worked there for a year and then pressured Papa to let me come to the Steak House thinking he would pay a little more. Wrong. I continued to make the same amount. I waitressed on weekends to make more money and continued to hate what I was doing. After getting married I finally found the courage to go back to school. After a couple of years, Papa agreed to lay me off (I think he was relieved) so I could collect unemployment while finishing my degree. The law allowed for me to collect without looking for work since I was already a full time student at the time of the lay off. I graduated with my teaching degree in 1989 and the rest, as they say, is history. I love education. I have never been bored and have always felt challenged and fulfilled. I'm planning to go back to school in January to get my principal's certificate.

I don't blame Papa. He did the best he could and he really thought he was doing the right thing. I felt pressured to make him and Nunny happy by going along. I also felt pressured to smooth the way for Ray [her brother] to come into the business. It took me a long time to break out of that "people pleasing" mold and to follow heart. Don't always make others happy, but I've learned that is their problem, not mine.

As for what was going on at the Steak House. The Eagle street ramp had closed at some time in the 80's and business got even worse. He filed the law suit that we eventually won after his death. I think the down slide of the business had begun before that. Papa refused to make changes on important things that could have made a difference. Beef prices were through the roof at that time and he was trying to make cuts in food cost by buying cheaper. Food quality was down. Leonard was a hack in the kitchen who had no creativity. Even if he had, Papa wouldn't allow it.

FROM THE BACK OF THE HOUSE

Just like Nunny [Evelyn Rose] refused to allow changes at the shop [her beauty shop] and it cost her the business. Anyway, that was when Papa started hanging out with that Pat woman and he started listening to her. He spent tons of money on remodeling when what he needed was to get rid of some of those crusty old waitresses and bartenders. Nice people in their own right, but not a plus for business. He over booked reservations and then made people angry when they had to wait. His health was deteriorating at the time as well as the stress and the lifestyle took its toll.

Don't misunderstand. I adored him and still miss him terribly. I think that if the business had continued to do well, that he would have been more open to change. He was very loyal to his employees, almost to a fault. He could be a real bastard, but he took care of them. I think that they were his family for a lot of years and while he loved us, he felt responsible for them . . . When Papa [Ray] called it a "baby that never grows up" he was absolutely right

There it is, reality sometimes a kick in the teeth, Ray steeped in "this is how it's always been done" (while taking a stab at the universal joke on humanity, immortality), got lost between limbo, bimbo, Gauguin, and Puerto Vallarta.

Alas, Cheri gone, Ray not knowing it (probably not wanting to know), turns out the new spring he envisioned wasn't a new spring at all, it was Indian Summer. And Indian Summer was about to end.

44

News Flash!

WEWS-TV broadcast the story March 30, 1986: "Flash, Flat's restauranteur found shot, killed, dead."

Well, maybe not the "killed, dead" part but true nevertheless.

Along with the story, WEWS-TV televised video of Jim's Steak House–the building, the big JIM'S sign, the works. Problem was, the dead person in question belonged to a different joint, namely DIAMOND JIM'S. A TV photographer had made an honest mistake. JIM'S is JIM'S the photographer figured, explained to his besieged boss.

Honest mistake or not, Ray freaked, sued.

The story in the Plain Dealer:

> Restaurant Owner Sues Over TV Item
> The owner of Jim's Steak House on Scranton Rad has filed a 1.8 million dollar libel and slander suit against WEWS Channel 5 in Common Pleas Court for loss of business due to what he said was a misleading newscast.
> Raymond Rockey, through his lawyer, Nicholas M. DeVito, said in the suit that on <u>March 30 last year</u> the station aired pictures of Jim's Steak House and reported the owner of Jim's Steak House had been killed and the business was closed.
> Rockey, who said he had operated his restaurant for 56 years, said yesterday that the station apparently got his restaurant confused with Diamond JIM'S Restaurant on Columbus Rd. The owner of that restaurant, James T.

FROM THE BACK OF THE HOUSE

> Vinci, 64, and a handyman, Edward Doubler, 36, were shot to death in Vinci's restaurant on March 30, 1985. The killing have not been solved. DeVito claimed in the lawsuit that because of the inaccurate broadcast, the restaurant lost business and substantial money. Rockey said people still came into the restaurant and told him they had heard he was dead.
> Don Webster, WEWS Station Manager, said he had not seen the suit and would not comment.
> The case was assigned to Judge Paul R. Matia.
> (The Plain Dealer, 2/27/87)

The reason it took Ray a year to file the suit, what would you guess–lawyer chit chat over a rum and coke, ladies in waiting . . . whatever, the suit was filed for 1.8 million dollars. That amount, if Ray had won, would have been bugled inside and out of not only JIM'S, but all around town. It didn't happen. Ray settled out of court, won in a backdoor deal the broadcasting business calls, "a trade." In short, in lieu of cash, Ray got "free" advertising time on WEWS-TV.

45
BELOW THE BELT

Ray's new spring turned Indian Summer got even more muddled when a Plain Dealer story, May, 1987, kicked him in the guts, some say lower. The story headline:

CLEVELAND UNEXPECTEDLY CLOSES EAGLE RAMP BRIDGE FOR IMMEDIATE REPAIRS

Eagle Bridge in permanent 'UP' as in closed

Overnight, Indian summer became winter. The most popular and easiest route (from downtown Cleveland to JIM'S) shut down, closed, kaput, the alternate way was some circumambulated one lane road past mounds of dirt, gravel, and a winding cow path that only Ray, Flat's truck drivers, a few hobo kings, and Indian ghosts knew of.

FROM THE BACK OF THE HOUSE

City Hall's icy lips on Ray's cheeks, he double freaked, sued everything east and west of the Cuyahoga. The legal battle (Jim's vs. Cleveland) started in 1987 would last, fester, and eat away at Ray for nearly seven years.

In the meantime, Ray drove around town in the JIM'S Van, nailing Jim's Steak House signs (with direction arrows to JIM'S) on utility poles. Some Cleveland manager muckity muck called and told Ray, the poles private property, he couldn't do that. He kept doing it.

Eagle Bridge closed, ongoing development of the Flat's (Nautica complex opened in 1987), more and more restaurant chains moving into the area, law suits, a young female server at JIM'S recalled, "We'd sit around at night, the place [JIM'S] was empty, Ray would lock up and we'd go uptown and drink."

Alas, the good years like a loved one in a nursing home begging to come home, but there is no home, Ray continued (to keep "baby" open) robbing Peter to pay Paul.

In it all–robbing Peter, suing City Hall, losing, appealing, losing, appealing–the muck took its toll. Add a long run of chasing panties, cat naps, fried potatoes, marbled meat, too much booze, and little molecules of fat, in Ray's already clogged arteries (he had had previous surgery for a plugged carotid artery some years earlier) piled up even more.

Nevertheless, he doggedly (another word is stubbornly) continued doing the only thing he knew to do, believed he was

FROM THE BACK OF THE HOUSE

meant to do: caring for "baby."

While we're here, might as well get to some short hair regarding the closed Eagle Bridge episode. By way of an intro, what is it they say about paranoia, it's not paranoia if someone is chucking *real* spears. It's when the spears are a figment of one's imagination . . . blah blah blah.

Suspicion, paranoia, or real, it always seemed a strange coincidence that Eagle Ramp bridge was "unexpectedly" closed in May of 1987 when, let's just say "other" Cleveland wired-to-city-hall muckety mucks (Nautica opened in '87), were developing the other end of the Flats.

One thing for sure (that duck thing, if it waddles etcetera), given politics, greed, and Mrs. Hubbards cupboard: if a bridge at the entrance to a wired-to-city-hall muckety muck's joint was in need of repair, it's a good bet on the duck's whatever it would not have taken nearly seven years (the bridge reopened December 17, 1993) to complete the bridge repairs.

And everybody said, "So what and who cares, it's like the last person killed in a no win war."

An observation from Authors John R. Wolfs and Sarah Ruth Wilson might shed some light: In *Bridges of Metropolitan Cleveland* (1981) they write of Cleveland, "The local government agencies are much too deeply infested by politics to be effective." (Chapter 7, page 92)

Alas, most everyone knows what (hint $$$) and who (those

FROM THE BACK OF THE HOUSE

who have $$$) drives politics. Goes way back to who got the warmest cave and bigger slice of mastodon. In short, in the land of nobody cares the movers and shakers have always figured out a way to steal legally.

Whatever, Ray Rockey never got into politics, never hobnobbed with the power brokers, never (far as we know) contributed to politicians. Ray was simply a party animal, a good time Joe, some say a playboy, some say other things. Whatever, he remained Peck's bad boy through it all. And like it always does, time and chance stuck a fat finger in the pie of fate and somewhere in when, what, and why things were meant to be, "my boy" ended up (after all those years when Aunt Hilda divined "my boy" to come out smelling like a rose) on the short end of the stick.

The legal battle (Jim's vs. Cleveland) really Ray vs. Cleveland, begun in 1987, back and forth, up and down, on November 21, 1994, a trial for damages to begin, the City filed a motion to dismiss. The trial court denied the motion as untimely. The jury found for the plaintiffs, awarding JIM'S $83,000 and Rockey $400,000 for lost rent, salary, and investment. The city appealed, maintaining that the court erred and for Ray, a setback printed in The Plain Dealer, March 15, 1996:

> Appeals court panel overturns a $483,000 award to Jim's Steak House Company that lost

FROM THE BACK OF THE HOUSE

business because of delayed bridge and ramp road repairs in the Flats; dismissal of an earlier suit by the restaurant barred it from filing again, three-judge panel says. *

Always be careful of "panel says." Next chapter.

---

*Blow by blow summary of the legal proceeding related to the JIM'S and the Eagle Street Bridge closing can be found at web sites:
<http://www-catalog.cpl.org/CLENIX?S=ROCKEY+RAYMOND+C>
<http://caselaw.lp.findlaw.com/scripts/getcase.pl?court=oh&vol=961211&invol=1>

46

THE END BEGINS

Beware of three things in life: sentences that begin with "Clearly," "Experts explain," and/or "Three judge panel says."

As related to the last, the society of smart lawyers and "three-judge panels" being whatever they are, the '96 Appeals court panel's decision was appealed anyway.

But sadly, the reversal process started, the end for Ray (like the shadow of an ugly stranger you thought you saw going around a corner but are not sure) had begun.

And you sensed, somewhere in his gut, Ray knew it when, seeing a giant oar boat ease by Collision Bend, he would get misty eyed.

Concerning oar boats and Ray being "misty eyed," years earlier Cleveland Press critic Winsor French noted the phenomena when he wrote:

> The Vernon Stouffers were at JIM'S the other evening . . . and were given quite a thrill when the huge ore boat, J. P. Morgan came around the bend, escorted by two busy little tugs . . . [Ray] Rockey was excited, too. He has the dimensions and statistics of all the freighters right on the tip of his tongue and likes to spiel them off. (Cleveland Press, July 1965)

So it was so at the end, "freighters" passing in the night, Ray communed, almost in a whisper, with them: "The William G. Mather, the Edward B. Greene, the H. L. Gobeille," like he wished he was on board, steaming to some new and

FROM THE BACK OF THE HOUSE

uncharted place, longing to find that long lost something.

In and around Ray's latter day freighter incantations, alternate life style males started to surface around JIM'S. The alternates often showed up in the penthouse. When I was visiting unexpectedly one evening, an alternate male, looking like he had just finished up with something, Ray straightening up his trousers, the former home of Hilda and Frank smelled like a pig farm. Like they say . . . stop. It's best left in the "maybe it was a dream" file.

Cheri (before she got "laid off," an on-the-spot eyewitness) put it this way, "A lot of things I could tell you, you really don't want to hear. It was not the greatest moral environment . . ."

In any case–a steady stream of Ray's stay overs, one nighters, two week stands, alternate life style pals, trips to Puerto Vallarta–things with Ray were becoming more and more switch-hitter bizarre as he played and preened and tried to keep it up. Old men do that, they look in the mirror, comb thinning hair and don't believe it isn't there. They look at the specks of dark speckled skin and don't believe it. They come from the bathroom with "I can't believe it" in their eyes. They silently say into your eyes, "How do I look." They wonder if the last time was the last time and thinking about it they worry they'll go blind.

Make a long story short, it didn't take a Dr. Jackerhoffer to see that Ray was one step from crossing that Tennyson bar.

47

By Pass

During this end time, on Friday night visits to *the* Steak House, Ray vented about his doctors, "I told them, it's $#% insane that I can't walk up the steps without getting winded."

In the middle of his harangues, a pack of smokes placed on the bar, he would take one and, when reminded about his health, uncork a cocky I'm-Ray-Rockey-Jim's-Steak-House look, strike a JIM'S safety match, and light up.

He didn't get it, or didn't want to, or did and wanted to.

A word about the I'm-Ray-Rockey-Jim's-Steak-House look that he flashed often, believed it mattered: One time at some Catholic Church benefit, along come then Ohio Governor, Richard F. Celeste. Shaking hands with everyone, Celeste got to our table. Ray didn't get up, just extended his right hand, they shook, and Ray said, "Ray Rockey, Jim's Steak House." The Gov. smiled and went on to the next hand.

At any rate, on one of the Friday night visits to *the* Steak House, Ray scheduled for bypass heart surgery in a few weeks, he looked forward to the procedure. Smiling, he joked that after the operation he'd have "new lead in his pencil." The way he smiled you could tell he believed he would be back in the saddle again. Confirming the belief, he had booked, shortly after the operation, another trip to Puerto Vallarta.

Alas, March,1993, a Monday, around 8:45 a.m., came an emergency phone call for yours truly. The caller a surgeon at

FROM THE BACK OF THE HOUSE

Metro Health, seems she had Ray split open neck to naval. Sounding like she might be sipping coffee, she explained that seldom had she seen such arterial flaking something or other (she didn't say something or other, some doctor term) in her life. She wanted to know if she should proceed. After a moment, we agreed Ray would want her to go forward.

Ten or so minutes later, came another phone call. Same surgeon reported that the flaking something or other in Ray's arteries scared the hell (she didn't say that) out of her but she did say she was concerned about clots, a stoke.

What can you say, I said, "Whatever you think."

As it turned out, she sewed him back up. No bypass.

That night, visiting in the dim light of Metro's intensive care unit, Ray lay in one of those metal beds, tubes everywhere. He opened his eyes, whispered, "Didn't go so good, huh."

Poor son of a bleep, you wanted to kiss him.

A few days later, sitting at JIM's cocktail bar, Ray just brought back from the botched bypass surgery, he took a cigarette from a stray pack on the bar. As before, he was reminded he wasn't supposed to do that. He flashed the old I'm-Ray-Rockey-Jim's Steak- House look and lit up.

Half way through a second drag, yours truly broached a health-related topic about having (some say it's important) the will to live, "You have to have the will."

Stopped cold, he bristled, "The will is done."

FROM THE BACK OF THE HOUSE

He obviously had other than the will-to-live in mind.

After a clarification, "I meant will, as in your will to live," he shrugged like he had stepped in something.

Clearly, he thought the mention of will was about his written will as in last will and testament in which, I found out later, I scored a goose egg or, as they say in tennis, love.

Anyway, bridge closings, law suits, appeals, competition, decline in business, third divorce, drinking, smoking, aborted bypass, it takes its whatever.

Amid it all Ray never gave up posting those JIM'S signs on utility polls around town. Eventually, he saw the opening of the Eagle Ramp bridge, December 17, 1993. They (a present from the city who evers) invited him to cut the ribbon.

Jim's STEAK HOUSE

48
THE CALL

The Eagle Ramp bridge finally opened, the seven-year battle with Cleveland bitter history, Jim's Steak House, like a

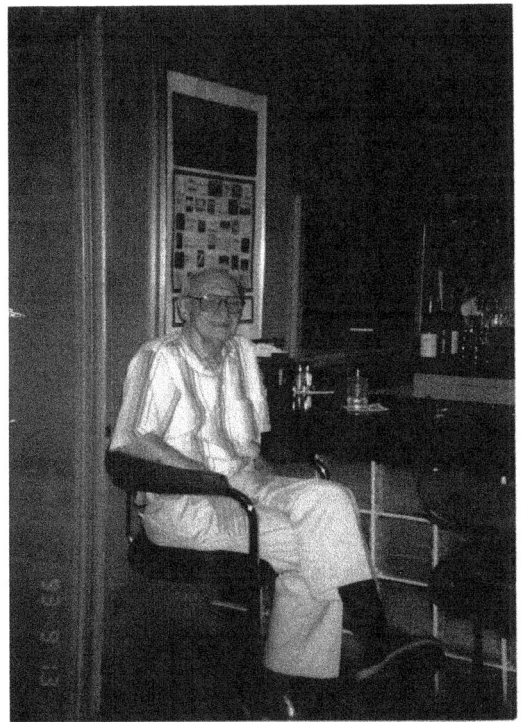

Ray at his favorite JIM'S bar perch

wounded animal with something shot away, would never be the same.

As to Ray, from his JIM'S perch on the end bar stool in the

FROM THE BACK OF THE HOUSE

cocktail lounge, he smiled in the twilight time of anticipation's promise of just one more.

Meantime, on Saturday mornings, the JIM'S "girls" regularly served him (as was his custom forever, in the main dinning room of JIM'S) breakfast. Coffee now replaced by tea flavored with a couple teaspoons of honey, there followed eggs, bacon, hash browns, and toast with plenty of real butter.

So much for butter, eggs, and bacon.

January 12, 1995, just thirteen months after the Eagle bridge had reopened, Ray, planning for his 72nd birthday (February 4) and yet another trip to his favorite frolicking spot, Puerto Vallarta, came the call.

To some "the call" is religious in nature. Like when one is called to some clothy position–priest, nun, preacher. To others "the call" has to with things theatrical, like "you got the part." Still others relate "call" to trading stock as in stock markets. And imbibers most certainly know about a bartender's "last call."

This "the call" was that other call. The one we all get about some relative, spouse, friend, somebody. The call, sooner or later, when somebody is calling someone about you.

Anyway, the call from wife Concetta* was short and to the point: "Your father died."

Forty five minutes later, yours truly arrived in the JIM'S penthouse. The kids (Cheri, Tami, Ray, and Karen) had already gathered. Nina, there too, she had found him in his

FROM THE BACK OF THE HOUSE

bed.

Stop.

Who is Nina?

Nina had become Ray's assistant/go-to lady in a long line flowing down from the Tony Liotta days. She filled in all around everything from waitress to hostess to making bank runs (taking cash to the bank). Living only a few miles away from *the* Steak House, she was on call at a moments notice.

The reason Nina found Ray: his current ritual (remember he was two steps short of robbing Peter to pay Paul) now involved, Monday through Saturday, 6:00 a.m., hobbling downstairs, unlocking JIM'S back door, letting the kitchen help in.

This particular morning, the back door locked, no Ray, the kitchen crew rang the door bell, banged, and finally telephoned Nina from a corner pay phone. Ten minutes later she arrived (she had a key), let them in, went upstairs to the penthouse, and made her way to Ray's bedroom. Her words, "I touched him, he was cold."

Anyway, the kids, Nina, yours truly standing around the death bed, a blanket pulled up to Ray's chin, his eyes closed like he was sleeping, his checkout wish had come true, "Just go to sleep, never wake up."

A quick rewind to earlier that morning: Around 5:30 a.m., hiking down our long home driveway to get the morning Plain

FROM THE BACK OF THE HOUSE

Dealer, passing a large pine tree (remember it was January), an icy spot, your truly flipped flat over tin cups. Never had done that before or since. What does that have to do with anything? Suspicion is that Ray, in that twilight time, tidying up loose ends this side of a long trip, had determined to get in one last shot before his final exit out of here. I swear the falling part is true, do what you want with the tripping.

Anyway, the kids, Nina, and your truly standing around Ray death bed, Father Joseph McNulty and Sister Corita Ambro (regular patrons at JIM'S for many years) from St. Augustine Catholic Church arrived. Father McNulty said a prayer, sprinkled some holy water, and shortly thereafter the Ripepi crew (Concetta had called, remember they were almost family) walked in.

The scene sticks in your mind like your first grade school teacher, first car, whatever—*Two Ripepi men wrap Ray's bed sheet around him, heft him onto a gurney, cover his face with the end of the sheet, wheel him down the back penthouse (around twenty) steps. Outside they slide him into the open end of a Ripepi hearse . . . .*

The Ripepi crew gone, the family agreed and Nina pasted a JIM'S CLOSED death notice on the front door. Something like: *Sorry, Due to the death of our Raymond Rockey, Jim's will be closed today.*

Next day, January 12, 1995, The Plain Dealer obit:

FROM THE BACK OF THE HOUSE

Raymond Rockey, longtime owner of Jim's Steak House

By MICHELE MELENDEZ
PLAIN DEALER REPORTER

CLEVELAND — For almost 50 years, Raymond C. Rockey did a little bit of everything at Jim's Steak House in the Flats.

"He cooked, washed dishes, talked to the people who came in, everything," his son, Gary Rockey of Hinckley, said. "It was his life."

Mr. Rockey started working at the restaurant full-time at age 24, after serving with the Coast Guard during World War II in Europe and the South Pacific as a radarman. When he left the service, he considered going to college under the GI Bill of Rights.

Meanwhile, he stopped by Jim's Steak House, then owned by his aunt, Hilda Mecurio, to help out for two weeks.

He never left.

Mr. Rockey, 71, died in his apartment above the restaurant yesterday.

He was born in Pittsburgh. During his school vacations, he would visit Cleveland and help out in his aunt's restaurant, which was named after her first husband.

He later moved to Cleveland and graduated from Benedictine High School in 1940, the year his aunt died.

After the war, he started working full time at the restaurant on the Cuyahoga River's Collision Bend. He became its manager in 1946. Soon after, the restaurant became his.

"The Flats haven't changed much since I was a boy," he told The Plain Dealer in 1968. "We served steaks from the start, and built that specialty to the point that we now serve a ton of steak a week."

Mr. Rockey moved into an apartment above Jim's so he could be close to the business.

"He'd open it up at 6 a.m. and stay there nearly all day," his son said. "He worked there up until the day before he died."

In 1984, his granddaughter, Cheri Rockey, joined the business after someone offered to buy it.

"When you've worked a lifetime to make something special, you're reluctant to turn it over to just anybody, no matter how much cash is involved," Mr. Rockey said. "When Cheri decided to come here, I couldn't have been more delighted."

Rockey

In 1992, Mr. Rockey sued the city for delaying repairs of the Eagle Ave. vertical lift bridge leading to the restaurant. He said a third of his business had disappeared because of the delay. A Cuyahoga County Common Pleas jury awarded him almost $500,000 last November.

"For years and years, Jim's supported me, but for the last six years, I had to support Jim's," Mr. Rockey told The Plain Dealer in November.

"He really loved that place," his son said.

Besides his son, Mr. Rockey is survived by four grandchildren and six great-grandchildren.

Services will be Monday at 10:30 a.m. at St. Augustine Catholic Church, 2486 W. 14th St., Cleveland.

Ripepi Funeral Home in Parma is handling the arrangements.

Thousands of former JIM'S customers and friends (Bob

FROM THE BACK OF THE HOUSE

Hulderman flew in from Sarasota) came to the viewing at Ripepi's on Pearl Road. After two days of viewing one of those bleak winter nights left a.m. Cleveland with a thick covering of snow (it had warmed up over night), fog, and slush a foot thick. Through the mist a hearse led the procession from Ripepi's to St. Augustine Catholic Church, W. 14th St where Father McNulty said mass. Then a blurred mile of vehicles made its way through the fog and mist to the Knollwood Mausoleum, 1678 S.O.M. Center Road. There, after Father McNulty said a brief eulogy, Ray joined Aunt Hilda and Uncle Frank in the family grotto wall:

I-unoccupied
II-Raymond Charles Rockey I
III-Uncle Frank
IV-Aunt Hilda

After the interment, Father McNulty announced one of those after the funeral luncheon at *the* Steak House. The joint packed, family had determined ahead of time, no booze. Reason: if there had been liquor, somebody might have had to call the next door Fire Station. So, white sheets covering the booze on the back bar, one old time JIM'S customer came up, exasperated frown on his face, said, "This is the first time in all my life I've been in Jim's Steak House and couldn't get a drink." He went away shaking his head.

Lunch finished, everybody gone, a brief what-next for JIM'S meeting with the kids and Nina. Consensus: Nina knew where the olive pits were stored, buried, kept. She would stay

FROM THE BACK OF THE HOUSE

on, continue to do what she had been doing. Yours truly would be manager.

And the next day they read "my boy's" will.

---
* In around 1983 stuff related to my first marriage hit the fan. Seven years later, at daughter Tami's wedding I met Concetta, something clicked, former Mayor Tomas Coyne of Brook Park, Ohio asked the "Do yous" and at this writing it's that many years later.

49
THE WILL

Some things (a good dinner, evening out, foreplay) are better stretched out, enjoyed. Others (common cold, flue, visiting in-laws) are best when shortened as much as possible.

The latter being the case regarding Ray's will, the short and sweet of it is this: what cash wasn't shot in the can by "my boy" when he "crossed over," he willed to yours truly's oldest daughter, Cheri.

A couple of possible self serving reasons for Ray's "left after" decision: Cheri, born in 1960, weaned at *the* Steak House, besides *the* Steak House, was the only baby (forget about blood) that Ray had ever known. Then again, maybe he never forgot yours truly dumping restaurant management at Michigan State, not telling him until he heard it third hand. Probably both but more than a little, maybe it was his peck's bad boy gotcha thing that got his goat.

Another comment along the lines of maybes: a few months after Ray's death, wife Concetta, upstairs in the penthouse cleaning, sweeping, dusting (we were running the place now, remember the after-funeral meeting agreement–we contemplated spending some nights there) became, for no apparent reason, falling down ill, dizzy, light headed, very sick. Rushed outside, breathing some fresh air, she felt better.

Next day the gas company was summoned to check the penthouse. A-oh. The carbon monoxide levels Mad Max

FROM THE BACK OF THE HOUSE

deadly, the gas company inspector found that the flu to the hot water tank in the laundry room had more holes rusted through it than Bonnie and Clyde's last ride.

What does this have to do with maybes? Recall, Ray, with a weak heart, went to bed in that lethal air just a few months earlier. No autopsy, we'll never know for sure but . . . you get the picture. One thing certain, if the carbon monoxide got him, and if what they say about an after life is true, Ray Rockey is spitting and spinning at the bugger of it all.

Maybe maybe maybe. If maybes were points in a football game everybody would win.

Whatever, the way it turned out, Cheri, the executrix of the estate, with the advice and help of legal council (her brother in law), divvied up whatever cash remained of Ray's inheritance * with her three siblings, yours truly, and her mother. She could have kept it all. There are many superlatives for her action, pick one.

As to Jim's Steak House, Inc., it was held by the estate with "the kids" (Cheri, Tami, Ray II, and Karen) along with the three daughters' husbands (Ray II not married) sitting on some kind of JIM's board of directors. The manager (that would be me) reported to the board. No snickering please.

---
*The final payout of the JIM'S law suit settlement and the later sale of the JIM'S building were handled (I had since resigned as manager) incognito and incommunicado to yours truly. It's another long story but the short and sweet is discussed later.

50

ARE YOU NUTS!

With regard to things long and short, short is best (trust me) when chronicling the last two years of JIM'S.

As mentioned above, after Ray's funeral the family huddled at *the* Steak House, decided Nina would stay on, yours truly would be manager reporting to the (also mentioned above) JIM'S board of directors.

Hello.

Turns out, not long after beginning the manager venture, some half baked disagreement over hiring Cheri's brother (yours truly's son, Ray II) hit the fan. Suffice it to say, it's another long story best left to read between the line.

Anyhow, my resignation in hand, the JIM'S board hired a college friend of a board member to run JIM'S. I had met the fellow months earlier at a family cook out and the thing that stuck in memory is that he used the "F" word at that gathering liberally. Something smelly in the wood pile to me, suggesting a vetting of him at my resignation board meeting seemingly self serving, I let it go. Subsequently the board decided to offer the college fellow a very attractive package (twenty thousand a year salary, rent free-living quarters in the penthouse, utilities, food and booze included) and he was brought on board.

The new manager's first assignment was to hire Ray II as executive chef of JIM'S.

FROM THE BACK OF THE HOUSE

You can see it coming.

Around six months later, planning a Friday night in downtown Cleveland for the kickoff to the Labor Day holiday, thinking it might be nice to nostalgia around with Concetta, have dinner at JIM'S, your truly called *the* Steak House for a reservation. No answer, nothing. Not even a machine message.

Wondering what's up, a call to daughter #2 board member brought a hesitation then a confession: She couldn't believe *the* Steak House was closed either. Seems the new manger had shut it down for Labor Day weekend, had other plans.

Figuring that smell in the wood pile had ripened, I said, "But it's the Flats, the pig ribs, the air show, the Tribe is playing at home, downtown is going to be packed."

"I know."

After assorted hems and haws, it was outed: a majority of the Board had had it with the new manager.

Not surprised, many things converging at that famous fork, wondering if all this is preplanned, free-will has anything to do with anything, yours truly and Concetta met with the unhappy JIM'S board to present a couldn't-be-refused-offer. The offer went like this: Concetta and I would take over running of *the* Steak House, keep it in the family, share profits, will it to "the kids" at our checkout.

Before the last sentence was dry, Cheri (executrix remember) said, "Where do we sign."

FROM THE BACK OF THE HOUSE

So much for "offers you can't refuse." The kids, now affiliated with in-law kids (one an attorney, one a CPA) one thing led to another and smack dab in a few weeks we were presented an umpteen page legal document titled, PURCHASE AGREEMENT, JIM'S STEAK HOUSE.

Bottom line, JIM'S Inc. (the restaurant business) would cost Concetta and me the amount "gifted" (when Cheri divvied everything up) to me after Ray Rockey checked out (around $35,000). We also would be obliged to pay the estate $500 a month for use of the JIM's building to operate Jim's Steak House.

My first reaction to the purchase agreement (Concetta more ballistic than over ill prepared calamari) unprintable, reading the contract again until the words wore out, I kept thinking it's a sign, don't' do it. With the thinking were my prayers to Xanadu for a ticket on a midnight train to Georgia.

Supplication to Xanadu unanswered, long and short of it, a week or so later, the JIM'S purchase agreement signed, a date set to take over, Cheri suggested Concetta and I take a short course (one day seminar) in running a restaurant.

This is not fiction.

Day of seminar there were maybe thirty people taking the course. The two guys running the show, wearing expensive looking suits, had (to yours truly anyway) a "You poor slobs," look on their faces before we started, after lunch, and the rest of the afternoon.

FROM THE BACK OF THE HOUSE

Anyway, proud new owners of Jim's Steak House, a shot at resuscitating underway, the first week, a former pal of Ray's, long time customer, local business man who Concetta knew and who knew the lay of the Cleveland business community, came in. A quirky look in his eye, he said to Concetta, "Are you nuts!"

51

EATING FREE!

Turns out the "are you nuts" guy was right. Namely, deep decay set in, the money needed for repair (the lease didn't cover building repair, shame on me) of the crumbling brick building, leaking roof, upkeep and replacement of ageing equipment made it a twit and a prayer every week just meeting payroll. Paying taxes, utilities, and vendors came in after payroll, twits, and prayers. Short and sweet, a cash ventilator would not have helped.

Adding to the excitement, before he left, the former manager fellow had signed JIM'S up with one of those entertainment coupon books–buy one get one free.

Ooops!

Get one free at burger's for a buck might work but not a steak dinner for $50.00 plus tips. As it turned out, JIM'S was packed but half were eating FREE!

In an attempt to stop the free coupon hemorrhaging, a notice was taped on the front door announcing that the coupons were no longer accepted. A few days later lawyers for the coupon company showed up and, after some haranguing, announced, "Contract is a contract, judge is waiting."

The sign came down.

Adding to all the good news, a Hilton Hotel size hot water take (installed during the 1950's remodeling by Uncle Frank, he hated running out of hot water when taking a shower),

FROM THE BACK OF THE HOUSE

serving both the restaurant and upstairs apartments, blew up. On top of that the kitchen scullers demanded a raise, the bartenders insisted on a clothing allowance, the "girls" wanted new uniforms, and the customer courtesy van needed new everything.

Topping off the good news, the land lease upon which JIM'S sat was due to expire end of the year, December 1996.

Skip back: remember that Forest City/Scranton Averell/Carter family three-step fandango when Scranton Averell bought the land under JIM'S; in the late 1980s things at JIM'S tight, Ray Rockey (to get a lower monthly lease payment from Forest City for the land upon which JIM'S sat) renegotiated the terms of the lease; "my boy" gave back years to keep JIM'S afloat . . .

Well, here we were, Fall of 1996, thinking JIM'S a Cleveland downtown landmark, optimistic that reason might prevail, umpteen attempts were made to negotiate a lease extension with Forest City. Numerous trips by Concetta and me were made to Forest City offices on the top floors of the Terminal Tower. Bottom line, squirreled in a squat conference room, meeting with a small army of tight-bottom Forest City suits and skirts we got shady smirks and smelly smiles like we might be droppings on new carpet.

We went over this before in an earlier chapter, but it bears repeating. Seems the tight-bottoms had pie in the sky plans for the Scranton Peninsula. The plans: on the coveted chunk

FROM THE BACK OF THE HOUSE

of Flat's dirt they envisioned quaint little shops, apartments, townhouses, a walkway with elevators and escalators so pedestrians could take a high rise stroll from Tower City over the Cuyahoga River to get to the quaint little shops and such.

Be that as it may, after many meeting, smirks, and smiles, the tight-bottoms offered a year to year lease. Alternate options: we could move the building or stick it.

Aside from the fact that a thousand Egyptian pyramid builders couldn't have moved that building, moving to a new location might have worked for a Ray Rockey restaurant-in-the-blood type but not here and now. To be real honest yours truly could never get excited about the cut of a loin of beef (except maybe to eat it), ounces of butter in a patty, counting empty liquor bottles, or unclogging grease traps. Not to mention other people's stomachs. See Chapter Two above, "ten reasons not to go into the restaurant business." Maybe that's why I never hit it off/bonded with Ray.

The whole thing made you want to sit right down and do something.

In any case, kinda like death rattles, in August of 1996, Joe Eszterhas' movie *Telling Lies in America* shot a couple scenes at JIM'S. Closed for one night for the filming, they paid around $5000.00 for lost business. It was a jinxed (maybe it was the *Lie* part) downhill ride from there.

Wanting out desperately but with no lease beyond a year,

FROM THE BACK OF THE HOUSE

no takers in sight, just when we thought you couldn't even give the joint away, along came a local group with connections to the then Cleveland political scene (never underestimate "backroom" political connections, see previous note about those who have $$$ driving politics.)

Presto. What was left of JIM'S Inc. sold in around November of '96 for about the same amount we paid the estate ("the kids") for it. In a sticky mess with "gazoutas" exceeding "gazintas," court filings, attorney fees, vendors paid off, the score again ended up "love" for the owners (that would be yours truly and Concetta) of Jim's. *

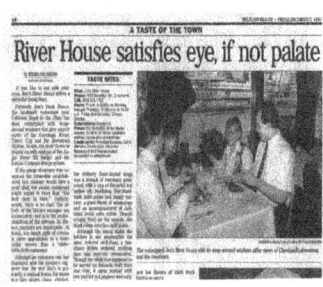

In the old Jim's Steak House building the new "local group with connections" (not privy to it, but assume the new group had some kind of land lease agreement with Forest City and a building lease with the Rockey Estate who still owned the building) premiered a joint called JIM'S RIVER HOUSE.

A short time after the new place opened a Plain Dealer review wasn't kind:

> If you like to eat with your eyes, Jim's River House offers a splendid visual feast. Formerly Jims' Steak House . . . if the group of owners who reopened the venerable establishment . . . would hire a good chef, the casual restaurant

FROM THE BACK OF THE HOUSE

might aspire to more than the best view in town. Unfortunately, there is no chef . . . the rough style of service is more appropriate to a blue collar tavern than a white tablecloth restaurant . . . the something for every palate principle seems overly ambitious . . . shellfish . . . so undercooked that the shells had not opened. . . . a luncheon sirloin ordered medium rare was severely overcooked . . . the steak was supposed to be served on foccacia with fries and slaw, it came instead with two pickled red peppers and salty home fries. The slaw that was belatedly delivered had been soaked in dressing so long that the cabbage had gotten soggy. . . after a long history as a popular family owned steak house . . . the owners need to make major improvements in the kitchen before the overpriced food compares with the million dollar view. (W. Salisbury, 12/5,1997, Plain Dealer)

That review, like telling someone in the hospital on life support, "You look pretty good," not only doesn't end up headlining grandma's scrapbook, it ends up in grandma's dumper. Not long after it opened, The River House closed. Another group took over, opened a nightclub for young adults, called it the Aqua. That closed in short order (I think somebody got stabbed but don't quote me), a third group painted the red brick building white, opened a dance something-or-other nightclub called MEGA which advertised among other things:

Thursday - sex night

FROM THE BACK OF THE HOUSE

Friday - social lounge night

Does anybody really want to know what Saturday nights offered.

Whatever, some say more than usual thunder clapped over downtown Cleveland in the months that the AQUA and MEGA operated. Others swear it was Aunt Hilda rolling in her Knollwood crypt, throwing things, knocking heads.

In any case, the white paint didn't help and the MEGA closed in less than short order. As of 2008, the surrounding Flats' land sets vacant as does the ghostly shell of Jim's Steak House. The basement (remember those sump pumps, electric, power turned off) flooded, windows broken out, pretty much a home for sea gulls and rats, the building is good for one thing–the demolition ball.

FROM THE BACK OF THE HOUSE

An AVAILABLE sign hangs on the front with some boating club using the dock space on the river. The Available sign number called, the whole ball of wax was available for lease from Forest City at around $8000.00 a month. *

So much for that, while downtown Cleveland dies, just a matter of time waiting for the uptown developer's to start (when they figure out a tax to pay for it) the envisioned shops and such.

---
*The Ray Rockey estate (the JIM'S board) at some point sold the building (out of the loop, don't know for how much) to Forest City who now owns the land, the building, the whole ball of wax.

Jim's STEAK HOUSE

EPILOGUE

Sans Everything

FROM THE BACK OF THE HOUSE

In 1946, when Ray Rockey was just twenty-three years old, Aunt Hilda made her "my boy" manager of JIM'S. Twenty-nine years later, 1975, Hilda died leaving Ray her empire. Ray, dumped into a sea of money, booze, and leading man status, the lid blew. Twenty years later, the empire pretty much shot in the can, Ray (just weeks short of his 72nd birthday, February 4, 1995) slipped away like he always said he wanted too, in his sleep. Less than two years later Jim's Steak House closed its doors forever.

As noted at the outset, in Shakespear's, "As You Like It," Jacques laments that all the world's a stage with players going through various ages from infancy to sans everything. Whether JIM'S was stuck in the infancy age (Ray's "baby" that never grew up) or not, for Ray Rockey the theater analogy fits.

In short, Ray Rockey liked the spotlight. Actually couldn't let go. Any why not? Think about it. Over the years, people have done some pretty nutty things to get, stay, and frolic in fate's fickle lime glow.

But unique to this show, Ray, unlike actors who, when the curtain goes up, playact for a time, "my boy" (disdaining "sack time," catching cat naps in a chair, on a sofa, sometimes in a bed)) playacted full tilt, 24/7, sixty minutes of every waking hour, some say nap time too.

And so it went, that Les Roberts' validation thing hounding him, the evening winding down, he'd say, "Time for a toddy for

FROM THE BACK OF THE HOUSE

the body." Working through more toddies than wee on a roller coaster ride, "my boy" stared in one long playhouse run. Dancing on some forgotten bliss, welcomed with open arms by Roquefort cheese groupies, he tiptoed (with an eye to some world record) though life and a mother lode of "panties."

Like Abe, a loyal and longtime JIM'S sculler often said, "When you die Mr. Ray, the good Lord ain't gonna owe you nuttin."

But it's anther long story and maybe not unique to owning a restaurant.

Then again, it may not be unique to any profession whose life style, floated in ninety proof booze, is obsessed with how much is left in the bottle and where the next one is coming from and "walking down there" with the young bulls to propagate the herd, even though you can't walk and, even if you could get there, all you find is not enough.

In short, Ray lost sight of the little things–leaking faucets, broken windows, dripping this and that, worn rugs, careless service and, as it turns out Ray's famous "baby" slogan was like the poet who don't know it.

Possibly shedding some light, Annie Dillard, reflecting on the subject of writing, notes " . . . [it's] like rearing children–willpower has very little to do with it. If you have a little baby crying in the middle of the night, and if you depend only on willpower to get you out of bed to feed the baby, that

FROM THE BACK OF THE HOUSE

baby will starve. You do it out of love. Willpower is a weak idea; love is strong. You don't have to scourge yourself with a cat o nine tails to go to the baby. You go to the baby out of love . . . "*

Whether true of writing or not, it's horseshoe close here. I.e., Aunt Hilda tended JIM'S out of love and it flourished. Ray Rockey, for some fifty years, with whiffs of attention from perfumed dolls (some guys too), bloated with faux fame and recognition, will powered his way around fickle-fate and free-will and the "baby" starved.

Whatever and in any case, Jim's Steak House a footnote in the long line of restaurants past, diehards insist that those Indian spirits forever hanging around Collision Bend had something to do with JIM'S demise. To this day many swear that the old JIM'S building is haunted. Whether it is or not, shortly after Ray died we found (cross my heart), in the basement and the penthouse laundry room, dead blackbirds. Big ones. No one knew how they could have gotten there. It's still a mystery.

Then there were extra busy nights when the restaurant toilets backed up and some at the bar swore they saw Indians out in the parking lot, dancing around a big fire, laughing their tee pees off.

One more: at the Steak House early one Sunday morning to count Saturday night's receipts, the place closed, there in

FROM THE BACK OF THE HOUSE

the kitchen alone, I saw Ray walking past the doors that led to the dinning room. Needless to say, no counting was done and I locked up and left immediately. The Sunday morning counting routine is fact. As in the tripping incident the day after Ray died, do what you want with the other.

While we're on ghosts and Indian spirits hanging around Collision Bend, the question arises, why else would they call it Collision Bend?

Think about it. Cuyahoga is Indian for crooked. Not only that, propelling Cleveland into the national "dump" spotlight, the river caught fire a few times. Bridges over it still get stuck. Boats, passing in the night, collide, run into its pilings. Then there's that rumored chat around the "why" table: Why didn't the Corp. of Engineers, at the time of the "unkinking"of Collision Bend in the early 1940's, cut a channel straight across the lower end of the Scranton Peninsula and thus eliminate Collision Bend altogether?

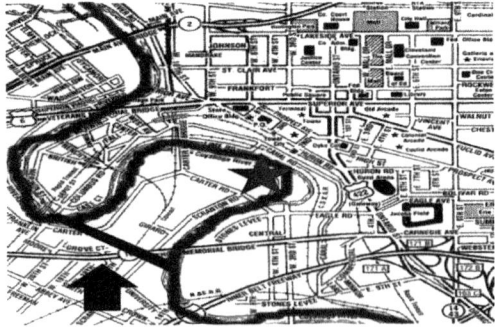

Star was JIM'S location, arrow points to the "what if" cut across Scranton Peninsula

FROM THE BACK OF THE HOUSE

Some suggest there had to be one or two back room Cleveland politicians involved. Politicians or not, ten to one, the Seneca, Chippewa, Mohawk (or some combination) ghost think-tank had something to do with it. Whatever, had Collision Bend been eliminated, the story of Jim's Steak House would have been . . . who knows.

Anyway, the blame game being what it is, lady luck's finger in the greater pot, JIM'S menus proudly proclaimed:

Cleveland's Original Steak Place Since 1930

Some sixty years later, the end of JIM'S didn't come (as Ray believed until the day he died), only because of the Eagle Bridge closing. No doubt the bridge closing was a final nail, but many things gone over ad nauseam led to JIM'S demise: resistance to change; new joints with fatter bank rolls; the obsession with cholesterol and how we play, drink, drive and second hand smoke.

There was a message printed (since they first came off the presses decades ago) on the back cover of the JIM'S menu that suggests (with talk of the crooked meanings in "Cuyahoga," "a place of wings," "lake river," "the wedding of a river and a lake") that those Indian ghosts really had any eye on the old place since the beginning:

FROM THE BACK OF THE HOUSE

JIM'S STEAK HOUSE
since 1930

When the Indian who named our river Cuyahoga looked on her for the first time, he saw a clear, sparkling stream, lazily meandering to the lake in the North. And all around him, almighty in its grandeur, a virgin wilderness attended her christening.

What he meant when he uttered "Cuyahoga" is something historians can't agree on. So we must choose from several interpretations.

First let's wander to the "Place of the Wing." Doesn't that suggest a refuge for wild birds in flight? Even today the Cuyahoga is such a haven. Not in the Flats to be sure, but up near her headwaters.

How about "Lake River?" We read its meaning as "the wedding of a river and a lake"... Cuyahoga and Erie.

But the Cuyahoga herself lends truth to the unromantic simple translation "Crooked." No one who has watched a 600 foot lake boat squeeze around Collision Bend can deny that Nature must have writhed in the throes of great indecision when she shaped the course of our river.

Perched on infamous Collision Bend, you'll find Jim's Steak House. Come down for dinner some evening and ask to be seated near a window looking out on the river. In the glow of soft light perhaps you will feel the romance of the Cuyahoga as we do. And though we can't command it, you may get a warm, friendly thrill as some ship's Captain plays his searchlight across our windows in greeting.

The Cuyahoga is crooked. She's a slave to industry. Yet down deep where her heart beats, she's pure and unsullied, and unashamed of her destiny.

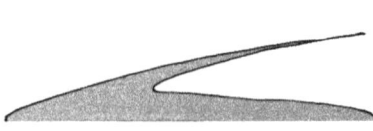

FROM THE BACK OF THE HOUSE

The last paragraph ends with a thought about the Cuyahoga: "... down deep where her heart beats, she's pure and unsullied, and unashamed of her destiny." Despite the validation demons, some think Ray Rockey was like that. No doubt about it, Aunt Hilda was.

In the end the City of Cleveland (that would be tax payers as opposed to the tight bottom muckity mucks) paid through the nose.

To wit: Ray's law suit against the City a slam dunk win is reported on the Devito law firm web page:

> ... VERDICT, DECISIONS AND SETTLEMENTS
> $483,000.00 Jury Verdict (Reinstated)
> January 28, 1998 (4 day trial)
> Ohio Supreme Court Case No. 96-1211
> Jim's Steak House, Inc., et al. v. City of Cleveland, 81 Ohio St.3d 18 (1998)
> The Ohio Supreme Court reinstated the 1994 jury verdict of $483,000.00 for the Jim's Steak House restaurant and its owner, Raymond Rockey against the City of Cleveland because it negligently closed the Eagle Avenue Bridge and reasonable access to the business for over six years. City of Cleveland eventually had to pay the Plaintiffs the entire judgment and post judgment interest on April 27, 1998 in the amount of $648,146.30.
> <http://www.mmd-law.com/devito1mmd.htm>

But it was too late for Ray. As noted above, he checked out, January 12, 1995.

For what it's worth, the estate reported around 40% of the

FROM THE BACK OF THE HOUSE

$600,000 plus judgement went for legal expenses. As it turned out, "the kids" got what was left and, maybe debunking who does what on whose grave, it's probably what "my boy" would have wanted.

---

*"To Fashion a Text," Inventing the Truth: The Art and Craft of Memoir, edited by William Zinsser. New York: Houghton Mifflin, 1987, 1998. 53-76

THE END

Restaurant Diner's
True/False/Depends Trivia TEST

FROM THE BACK OF THE HOUSE

TEST

1. You can tell, when you're served a steer steak, if it's from a bullock or a steer.

2. A bullock's mooing is higher pitched than cows.

3. Getting slammed is what professional wrestlers, male and/or female, get.

4. Getting slammed is when a restaurant gets more customers than it can handle.

5. There is eight ounces of fat in a one once patty of butter.

6. Short ribs come from male cattle so do steer stakes, T-bones, NY strips, rib eye, and prime rib.

7. Hamburger comes from cows.

8. Prime, choice, and DNA are government terms for beef.

9. The more marbling in beef, the higher the "good" government rating.

10. Marbling refers to the amount of fat in a piece of meat, the more marbling the more tender, the less marbling the more chew.

11. Chewing is good for you.

12. Ham steak is pork dressed up for dinner.

13. Blue cheese salad dressing is the same as Roquefort salad dressing.

14. Gorgonzola is blue cheese.

FROM THE BACK OF THE HOUSE

15. Splitting tips began in 6010 B.C..

16. Up is a glass of water on the side with a shot of booze.

17. Up is a shot of booze.

18. Up can also be eggs as in sunny side.

19. Up yours is a side order of up.

20. A jigger is a bug.

21. A jigger is a metal utensil for measuring quarter and half ounce shots of booze.

22. Rare, medium rare, medium well, and well done are fictional terms used in men's magazines.

23. A round hamburger tastes the same as a square hamburger.

24. A round top is a table.

25. A four top is a table for four.

26. A deuce is a table for two,

27. Stiffed refers to tips, as in none to little.

28. A cocktail can be food or booze.

29. Top shelf booze is the good stuff, usually on display on the back bar.

30. Well liquor is the cheap stuff, usually in a metal tray around the bartender's knees.

31. Soup of the day is yesterday's whatever.

FROM THE BACK OF THE HOUSE

32. Surf and turf has something to do with a beach.

ANSWER KEY: True/False/Depends
1. D
2. D
3. D
4. T
5. D
6. D
7. D
8. F
9. T
10. T
11. D
12. D
13. D
14. D
15. D
16. D
17. D
18. T
19. D
20. D
21. T
22. D
23. T
24. D
25. T
26. T
27. T
28. T
29. T
30. T
31. D
32. D

 JIM'S RECIPES

FROM THE BACK OF THE HOUSE

STEAKS
Steaks should be liberally marbled. What is that: Marbling: the grains/streaks of fat running through meat. This is what makes the strips, T bones etc. flavorful, tender. It's the fat that does it, if you don't like fat, chew it. Filet is naturally tender because it is a muscle that get little to no exercise. It is also not fatty, can be dry especially when over cooked as in well done that's why they wrap it in bacon sometime.

Cooking steaks – Grill should be smoking hot. Salt and pepper after putting on grill, let cook, flip, salt pepper other side. Rare, press meat if it feels like the soft place in you palm just below your thumb it is rare. If it feels like the sole of your shoe it is well done.

JIM'S HASH BROWNS
Boil potatoes in jackets until fork tender. Drain and let set until room temp. Scrape jackets off potatoes. Dice, put in cooler. Render beef fat. Cook potatoes in liberal (half cup fat for single portion) amount of the rendered fat until golden brown, flip and do other side. Add some more rendered beef fat. Serve hot. Salt to taste. Call your cardiologist.

JIM'S ONION RINGS
Slice onions and separate into rings. Dredge rings in flour, then in an egg wash (beaten eggs & milk), 3-4 eggs/cup of milk, then dredge in cracker meal. Deep fry in rendered beef fat until golden brown. Be sure fat is hot, test by dropping a small piece in, if it begins to fry immediately, grease is hot enough. If not, onion rings will soak up to much grease. Can keep breaded onion rings in fridge for 2-3 days. Best when done fresh as onions become limp after a day or so. (Courtesy of Cheri)

JIM'S Salad Dressings:
French (note this is restaurant portion mix)
8 cups sugar
1 ½ cup paprika

FROM THE BACK OF THE HOUSE

1/8 cup salt
2 cups oil, vegetable
3/4 gallon white vinegar
3 gallons plain mayonnaise
mix all ingredients well, place in gallon plastic containers in frig. Put in 1 cup salad dressing bowl when served
Thousand Island
 Add 1 pint pickle relish to 3/4 gallon French dressing recipe
Roquefort
Crumple hand full of blue cheese in a quart of French dressing recipe

Cleveland/Jim's Time Line

See Cleveland
from the
TERMINAL TOWER
708 FEET HIGH

FROM THE BACK OF THE HOUSE

1796 - Moses Cleaveland lands a survey party on the east bank
1797 - The Lorenzo Carter family first settlers on the east bank near Superior Avenue
1814 - Cleveland incorporated as a village
1825 - The first permanent bridge is built at Center Street
1830 - The rivalry between Cuyahoga east-bank Cleveland and west-bank Ohio City erupts
1832 - The Ohio & Erie Canal from Cleveland to the Ohio River is opened
1837 - The Bridge War is fought between Cleveland and Ohio City
1854 - The west side of the river becomes a part of Cleveland
1870 - The first Standard Oil Company refinery begins production
1873 - Sherwin Williams opens first paint factory on Canal Street
1878 - The Superior Viaduct, Cleveland's first high-level bridge is opened
1892 - The Powerhouse in the Flats built by Marcus Hanna to supply electricity for streetcars
1898 - Work begins to re-channel and widen the mouth of the Cuyahoga river
1899 - Hilda Theresa (Hoffman) Kerkles/Mercurio born
1905 - James Kerkles arrives New York from Greece
1918 - Veterans Memorial Bridge opens. Streetcars travel the bridge's second deck
1920 - Indians win World Series
1923 - Ray Rockey and Evelyn Rose (Ferra) Rockey born
1923 - James Kerkles and Hilda T. Hoffman married
1930 - Republic Steel is founded by Cyrus Eaton
1930 - First JIM'S opens near 1149 W.9th St, Cleveland
1931 - Lumbermen's club moves to Terminal Tower complex
1931 - JIM'S moves to lumbermen's club in the Flats
1932 - Lorain-Carnegie Bridge (Hope Memorial Bridge) is opened
1938 - Ground is broken in for the Main Avenue Bridge
1939 - March, Collision bend unkinking announced

FROM THE BACK OF THE HOUSE

1939 - Four months later James Kerkles dies June 15, 1939
1940 - Frank Mercurio doing construction work for new JIM'S location, meets Hilda
1941 - JIM'S moved back 125 feet to new location 1800 Scranton Road
1941 - Ray Rockey and Tony Liotta graduate Benedictine High School
1941 - Collision Bend widening completed
1942 - Ray Rockey enters Coast Guard
1944 - Ray Rockey discharged from Coast Guard, goes to work full time at JIM'S
1945 - Ray's first marriage, divorce short time later
1946 - Hilda and Frank marry, first house on Pleasant Valley
1946 - Ray is made manager of JIM'S
1948 - Evelyn Rose Ferra moves to Cleveland, job at JIM'S, Indians win second World Series
1951 - Evelyn Rose and Ray Rockey marry
1952 - Winsor French article critical of JIM'S
1954 - Evelyn Rose's son Gary adopted by Ray Rockey
1955 - Frank and Hilda build penthouse above Jim's
1956 - Carters offer land under JIM'S, Hilda takes lease instead, Scranton-Averell buys land
1957 - Second Windsor French article critical of JIM'S, remodeling starts
1958 - The new JIM'S Seaway room opens
1959 - Aunt Hilda's willow tree damaged
1960 - Charlotte (Ray's third wife to be) enters
1962 - Evelyn leaves, separation, divorce, Charlotte era begins
1963 - Aunt Micky dies
1972 - Charlotte leaves, separation
1974 - Hilda dies, Charlotte returns for short time.
1975 - Frank Mercurio Sr. dies, Charlotte/Ray divorce
1976 - The Flats Oxbow Association is founded, Flats becoming entertainment center
1981 - Sammy's opens in the flats
1983 - Cheri graduates from CIA

FROM THE BACK OF THE HOUSE

1986 - March 30, WEWS-TV mistakenly reports death of JIM'S owner, Ray sues
1987 - The Nautica entertainment area opens on the west bank
1987 - Eagle Ramp Bridge closes
1989 - The Powerhouse reopens as an entertainment complex
1992 - The Rose Iron Works on the east bank is renovated and opens as an entertainment center
1993 - December, Eagle Ramp Bridge reopened
1994 - Jacobs Field opens for Indian's baseball
1995 - January 12, Ray Rockey dies
1996 - Cleveland cerebrates bicentennial
1996 - December, JIM'S closes

FROM THE BACK OF THE HOUSE

END NOTES

THE ENCYCLOPEDIA OF CLEVELAND HISTORY
http://ech.cwru.edu/

1.) The CLEVELAND PRESS was the flagship of the communications chain founded by EDWARD W. SCRIPPS. Five years after helping his brother James start the *Detroit News,* Scripps came to Cleveland, where he started the *Penny Press* on Frankfort St. on 2 Nov. 1878. A small, 4-page afternoon daily, it reflected Scripps's predilection for news condensation and announced its independence of party politics. Although Scripps relinquished personal direction of the *Penny Press* within 3 years, the paper continued to prosper. Its name was shortened to the *Press* in 1884, and it finally became the *Cleveland Press* in 1889. By its 25th anniversary in 1903, the *Press* was Cleveland's leading daily newspaper. In 1913 the *Press* moved into a new plant at E. 9th and Rockwell (the present BancOhio Bldg. site). As it entered the 1920s, the *Press* neared 200,000 in circulation and maintained its political independence by proposing the city manager form of government for Cleveland and supporting Progressive candidate Robt. La Follette for president in 1924. LOUIS B. SELTZER became the 12th editor of the *Press* in 1928, and under his 38-year stewardship the *Press* became one of the country's most influential newspapers. Seltzer readjusted its original working-class bias into a less controversial neighborhood orientation, stressing personal contacts and promoting the slogan "The Newspaper That Serves Its Readers."
In the postwar period the *Press* continued its public service campaigns and remained an unrivaled force in Ohio politics, as demonstrated by its successful promotion of FRANK J. LAUSCHE and Anthony J. Celebrezze as mayors of Cleveland, and the former as governor of Ohio. In 1954 the *Press* played an aggressive, controversial role in the prosecution of Dr. Sam

Sheppard for the 4 July murder of his wife, Marilyn, in their Bay Village home (see SHEPPARD MURDER CASE). The *Press* maintained its preeminence in the city and state through Seltzer's retirement in 1966. It moved into a modern printing plant at Lakeside and E. 9th in 1959 and 1 year later purchased the CLEVELAND NEWS from the FOREST CITY PUBLISHING CO., merging it into the *Press* and thereby becoming the city's only surviving afternoon daily. In 1964 the *Press* was named one of America's 10 best newspapers in a list compiled by *Time* magazine. Under Seltzer's successor, Thos. L. Boardman, however, the *Press* began a decline that was shared in general with other large afternoon dailies throughout the country. Circulation was down to around 300,000, the *Press* having surrendered its lead to the morning *PLAIN DEALER* in 1968. Shortly after Boardman's retirement in 1979, rumors began circulating that the *Press* would shortly suspend publication unless it could be sold. Scripps-Howard sold the paper on 31 Oct. 1980 to Cleveland businessman Joseph E. Cole, who had exacted concessions from 9 *Press* unions prior to the purchase. In an effort to restore the paper's competitive position, Cole introduced a Sunday edition on 2 Aug. 1981 and a morning edition on 22 Mar. 1982. Citing the depressed economy and consequent losses in advertising, however, Cole announced the paper's closing on 17 June 1982, and the final edition appeared that afternoon. The former *Press* plant was demolished to make room for the North Point office complex.

http://ech.cwru.edu/
The Encyclopedia of Cleveland History

2.) FRENCH, WINSOR (24 Dec. 1904-6 Mar. 1973), society columnist for the CLEVELAND PRESS, was born in Saratoga Springs, N.Y., to Winsor P. and Edith French. He became the stepson of Joseph O. Eaton, founder of the EATON CORP., after his father's death. French moved to Cleveland with his family in 1915. After sporadic education, he worked for the

FROM THE BACK OF THE HOUSE

CLEVELAND NEWS and TIME. In 1933 he joined the *Press* and married Margaret Hall Frueauff. A year later Mrs. French obtained a divorce, becoming a noted actress under the name Margaret Perry.
French wrote some drama criticism for the *Press*, but found his calling as a society reporter. His friends included Lucius Beebe, Marlene Dietrich, Clark Gable, Libby Holman, John O'Hara, and Cole Porter. He left the *Press* to live in New York in 1941 but returned at the conclusion of WORLD WAR II. Sent to Europe to report on the condition of the average European in 1946, he cabled interviews with Noel Coward, Beatrice Lillie, and Somerset Maugham. Never remarried, French lived like the people he wrote about partly through the gift of IBM stock from Clevelander Leonard Hanna. Failing in health and confined to a wheelchair late in his career, French campaigned for the rights of the handicapped, resulting in Mayor Ralph Locher ordering City Hall and other city buildings to be made accessible to handicapped persons, and in French's receiving a presidential citation in 1966. He retired from the *Press* in 1968, and is buried with his parents in Williamstown, Mass.

http://ech.cwru.edu/
The Encyclopedia of Cleveland History

FROM THE BACK OF THE HOUSE

About the author

By way of Carnegie Mellon Drama Department, G. L. Rockey earned a B.A. from Michigan State University and entered the television industry. From Providence to Phoenix and cities in between, he produced and directed a variety of television programs and managed TV station programming. Awarded a Master Degree, he taught at Cleveland State University.

From the Back of the House his first non-fiction book, Mr. Rockey has written three novels: *Time and Chance, The Journalist, and Truths of the Heart*. An anthology, *Bats in the Belfry, Bells in the Attic,* is a collection of sixteen off the wall short stories. Rockey is at work on a fourth novel.

Keyword: G. L. Rockey
Web page: www.glrockey.com

www.ingramcontent.com/pod-product-compliance
Lightning Source LLC
Chambersburg PA
CBHW050333230426
43663CB00010B/1840